Easy Poetry Lessons

That

Dazzle & Delight

SCHOLASTIC
PROFESSIONAL BOOKS

NEW YORK • TORONTO • LONDON • AUCKLAND • SYDNEY

EDITOR'S NOTE:

Four years ago David Harrison and Bee Cullinan decided to write a book together, going on the hunch that their different perspectives—that of a poet and of a teacher—would complement each other nicely. But they quickly discovered in this arranged marriage of authorship that their views on teaching poetry were remarkably different—and that they sometimes clashed. Bee favors free verse and questioned introducing too many details of structured verse to children, while David doggedly defended his belief that teaching iambic pentameter and the like wouldn't turn children into staunch poetry phobes. Faxes, Fed-Exes, and phone calls flew back and forth between the three of us, revision upon revision towered like stacks of Saltines in our offices. Teachers were called upon to read drafts and give their views. Poems and lessons were added, deleted, tweaked, and debated until days before the production deadline. In the process, we reexamined our beliefs about teaching poetry and wound up with richer, broader perspectives. And in the end, Bee and David wrote a book that offers an eclectic mix of their sensibilities. This is its beauty and its strength. Too often in educational publishing we deliver one school of thought on a topic, and tune out others. Working with Bee and David taught me a lot about the wisdom of editing with an open mind and about the power of sticking to one's convictions. Their passion as educators and poetry lovers is remarkable, and it produced a fine book. (And a whopping strain on my fax machine.)

—Wendy Murray, editor

Front cover design by Kathy Massaro
Interior design by LDL Designs
Interior illustrations by Julie Durrell

0-590-12050-6
Copyright © 1999 by Berenice E. Culinan and David L. Harrison
All rights reserved.
Printed in the U.S.A.

Dedications

To all teachers and poets who are handing down the magic—a love of melody in language. —*BC*

To my mother, for writing letters in couplets and teaching me the Gettysburg Address. Thank you. —*DLH*

Acknowledgments

I thank my teachers and friends: Charlotte S. Huck, Shelley Harwayne, and Nancy Larrick. My Writers Group: Joie Hinden, Joan Irwin, Ann Lovett, Marilyn Scala, Ginnie Schroder, and Deborah Wooten. My students: Audrey Risden, Nance Wilson and their colleagues. Poets I have known: Brod Bagert, Allan DeFina, Rebecca Dotlich, Aileen Fisher, Ralph Fletcher, Kristine O'Connell George, Monica Gunning, Georgia Heard, Juan Felipe Herrera, Lee Bennett Hopkins, Joy Hulme, Karla Kuskin, J. Patrick Lewis, Lillian Morrison, Alice Schertle, Eileen Spinelli, Michael Strickland, Janet Wong, Jane Yolen, and especially David Harrison who made the journey of writing this book an exciting and surprise-filled, joyous trip. —*BC*

I thank the following teachers who kindly read early drafts of this book and provided valuable insights and advice: Dixie Neyer, Vicki Newport, Kathy Holderith, Nelda Silva, Nancy Raider, Jennifer Jackson Harrison, Suzanne Houghton, and Michael Gravois. —*DLH*

Table of Contents

Foreword

In this book you are invited to view poetry through the eyes of a poet and the eyes of a teacher. The poet, David Harrison, has published forty-six children's books and spent a lifetime relishing words and poetry. The teacher, Dr. Bernice (Bee) Cullinan, is a professor emeritus of Early Childhood and Elementary Education at New York University and editor-in-chief of Wordsong, the poetry imprint for Boyds Mills Press, to name just two of her many outstanding roles in education.

Both David and Bee know first-hand that studying poetry is an exciting and efficient way for students to learn about language. A poem is a whirring, chugging model of the English language—and kids love models. They enjoy the sense of control that comes with rearranging doll houses, commanding toy action figures and directing computer games. Similarly, with a poem, a student can attend to each word, each syllable, each sound. Its small size makes it perfect for close study and invites experimentation. A poet can rearrange every line, or change all verbs from past tense to present tense in a minute, and then watch how the poem responds.

A finished poem has a physical quality—like a small sculpture, a tiny machine, a lovely music box—with its own shape and size and visual design. You can hold it in your hand, carry it in your pocket. But the poem also has the ethereal quality of a song: You read it aloud, and it lingers in the listener's mind.

In ...*Dazzle and Delight*, Bee and David show you how to teach kids about the structure and the "song" of poetry. Their strategy lessons explore the music of *alliteration, assonance,* and *consonance* and why these techniques create a resonance in the poem that further echoes the words' meanings. They also introduce the formal rhythmic patterns that have evolved in the history of poetry and provide activities that invite children to enjoy these patterns without feeling intimidated. David and Bee have selected poems that put kids at ease—there's enough silly verse, from nonsense poems to loopy limericks, to keep kids from thinking that poetry is stodgy stuff for grown ups.

In addition to metrical patterns for poems, Bee and David cover several poetic forms specifying numbers of lines and rhyme schemes. They examine free verse and rhyming poetry. Just as classical music and jazz use the same notes and instruments to create dramatically different moods and sounds, free verse and rhyming poems use the same words to invent distinctly different poetry. Some poetry lovers are passionate in their preference for one form or the other; through the activities in this book, students can explore the challenge and experience the satisfaction involved in creating a poem in either form.

Bee and David devote the first chapter to the voices and ideas of teachers across the country, who share their favorite ways of celebrating poetry in their classrooms. From there, the strategy lessons proceed. David begins each lesson with a BACKGROUND discussion in which he shares anecdotes and his personal approach to a specific aspect of poetry. Illustrated reproducible poems demonstrating the poetic form or technique accompany each lesson. The lessons have two parts: an engaging TWO-MINUTE WARM-UP and a challenging ACTIVITY designed to involve students immediately in exploring the specified technique while writing their own poetry.

The study of poetry provides a rare opportunity for you and your class to have fun together while learning valuable lessons about language and about each other. Poetry opens students up to a heightened sensitivity to language that carries over into all reading and writing. You can be sure your students will be interested in the subject matter—it's all about them. And poetry offers them a dynamic way to express their thoughts and feelings. The first line of this Foreword invited you to view poetry through double lenses—that of the poet and the teacher. As you travel now with your students through these lessons—these adventures in poetry—you may find yourself moving to the beat of a double rhythm—that of the English language and the human heart.

—*Steven Aldridge, poet, New York City, February, 1999*

CHAPTER 1:
Creating a Poetry-Rich Classroom

The truth: There is no one right way to teach students about poetry. In the following pages, teachers from across the United States share their tips and inventions and offer some ideas to get you started. Take these suggestions, adapt them for your students, and you will be well on your way to cultivating a poetry-minded classroom.

SURROUND KIDS WITH POETRY

The best way to create a poetry environment is to surround students with poetry—on the walls, in the halls, in the air, everywhere.

Surround students with the sounds of poetry. Read it every day! Choose poems that are silly or serious, long or short, a cry from the heart or nonsense. Students should be immersed in poetry. Invite poets to the school to read their own poetry. Let students read poetry in unison and individually.

Read Aloud Often
Sandra Brand, Fourth-Grade Teacher, Academy School, Madison, CT
In my own class I read a lot of poetry out loud, enjoy the natural rhythm and song of the language, and ignite a desire to write poetry. The reading of fine work, both silly and serious, allows kids to feel comfortable in creating their own pieces. I tell them that poetry is easier to write than

prose because you aren't constricted by the conventions of sentence, paragraph, etc. The message is that poetry needn't rhyme, but may; that your mission is to present a really fine painting or picture using the most perfect word brush; and that you must not push the rhyme, the image or the language. The balance of all these is like an image suspended in time—one that only you could describe, but one that all of us can visualize because of the words you have chosen.

Match Up Poetry With Classical Music

Deborah Wooten,
Fifth-Grade Teacher,
Glenwood Landing School,
Glen Head, NY

I play classical music softly in the background while my students are reading poetry, writing poetry, or writing responses to poetry. I choose music related to the topic or period we are studying. For example, if we are studying the early 1800s, I choose music by Wagner (1813–1883) or Verdi (1813–1901). Sometimes I choose poets and musicians who had similar lives or traits, such as Edgar Allen Poe (1809–1849) and Mozart (1756–1791), who were poor, lonely, and led tragic lives. Sometimes I choose music that is in keeping with a particular activity. When I read sleep poems I play Strauss lullabies. When I read Walt Whitman I play music from the Civil War period. Students love it, stay focused, and work hard.

Create a Poetry Corner
Collect materials related to a poem topic students will write about: Signs of Fall (leaves, twigs, acorns, nuts, pumpkins, squash, Indian corn, Halloween masks), Spring Is Here (buds, sprouts, insects, blossoms, tulips, Easter eggs, spring bonnets), Ocean and Seashore (sand, sea shells, seaweed, boat sounds, smells, water, fish, aquariums). Supply plenty of information on the topic as well as topic-related poetry books.

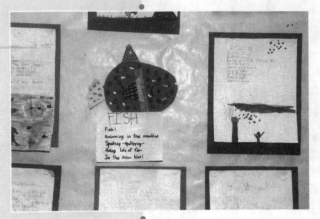

Put on a Grand Celebration

Doug Russell, Third Grade Teacher, Echo Horizon School, Los Angeles, CA

Students in our two third-grade classes spend about nine weeks thoroughly immersed in poetry in the fall of each year. We begin with the teachers reading several examples of poetry to help students see how the author uses words in many different ways to create mental pictures and sometimes tell a story. Humorous poetry is always popular. Shel Silverstein and Jack Prelutsky are a hit; they get everyone involved. Following a general introduction to poetry, the teachers read examples of a particular style of poetry, such as haiku or limericks. We have the students discuss the characteristics of that form and write several poems of that type. We usually study eight to ten different types of poems.

During this process, the students are encouraged to read poetry on their own during independent reading time both in class and at home; soon, they are bringing in and sharing poems they particularly enjoyed. Part of the culmination of the poetry unit is a class anthology of five or six of each student's poems. Many pen and ink drawings by the students are included to illustrate the poetry. The anthology is reproduced so that each student will have a copy with his own original artwork on the cover of the book he takes home. They also host a very formal poetry presentation for the parents on the day before Thanksgiving vacation. The students select two of their published poems to present. Since it is a formal event, they must wear "dress up" clothes. They each have their turn to stand at the microphone on the lectern. Class choral responses to each of the poems, usually quite amusing, provide whole class involvement throughout the presentation as well as audience involvement as each student is returning to her seat.

The presentation is a grand celebration of poetry, individual student creativity, and total class effort in putting the project together.

Following the presentation is a very formal reception hosted by the room parents for both students and parents with hors d'oeuvres and sparkling cider. The final part of the culmination is a videotape of the presentations which students may keep to enjoy for many years to come. The presentation is a wonderful adventure that integrates many of the facets of the language arts program at our school.

A Twist on Tongue Twisters

Julie McGovern, Resource Teacher, Speech and Language Specialist, Echo Horizon School, Los Angeles, CA

The second- and third-grade students with whom I work are hearing impaired, so our focus is on speech and language. I select poems which emphasize the speech targets we are working on. We pay particular attention to speech duration, intensity and pitch, and presentation style. I generally pick silly and humorous poems, frequently from Shel Silverstein, to keep the sessions lively and interesting. I also use tongue twisters. These focus on my student's specific speech targets and emphasize rapid repetition. To increase involvement and interest in this area, students create individual books of original tongue twisters. They illustrate these with the help of computer software and have their own copies of the meaningful material for reading and speech rehearsal.

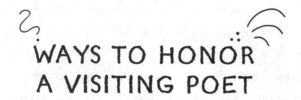

WAYS TO HONOR A VISITING POET

Communicate with a poet. Poets live everywhere, and they like to communicate with students who read their poetry. Go to the public library to find poets who live near you. Invite a poet to your school. Some poets have a web site. Get on the Internet. Track down information about poets you like. Some poets will hold a conference call with a group of students. Contact their publishers to find when poets may be doing school or bookstore visits in your area. There are many poets who are not published, but they enjoy reading from their work. Students can learn from them, and the poets benefit from student response to their work. Ask around at local colleges or writing groups. Volunteer your class as a field test group for a promising poet in your neighborhood.

Poet Rebecca Dotlich enjoys a student's recitation of one of her poems.

Memorize Poems to Recite

Pat Werner, Third Grade Teacher, Manhattan New School, New York, NY

In advance of a poet's visit, have each student pick one of the poet's poems to memorize. Before Rebecca Dotlich visited us, my students started by copying the poems they'd chosen onto index cards. On the back I asked each child to write about why they chose that poem and to really think about what made it special for them. We practiced reading one of Rebecca's poems on the overhead, emphasizing the line breaks and stanza breaks with long pauses. They loved the challenge of reading the poem as Rebecca herself might.

Every day children begged to practice their reciting of Rebecca's poem. They had chosen the most rhythmic to recite, and it was fascinating to discover that they made the poems their own, so much so that they started to think of new words they liked even better. For example, one student liked "silver of moon" better than the poet's "sliver of moon." They were really tuning into poetic language. I had not realized that memorizing a poem would lead to so much additional learning. And, of course, when the children each recited a poem to Rebecca, it moved her to tears.

Two students perform a rap version of Rebecca's poem.

February 2, 1999

Ms. William's Kids
Eldon Upper Elementary
313 E. 15th Street
Eldon, Missouri 65026

Dear Kids,

You're right. We are going to have fun. I love your letters and am sleeping with them under my pillow every night. Except Wednesdays. That's the dog's night to sleep under there. Next time I'm getting a flatter dog. This one's all lumpy.

Courtney, I'm looking forward to hearing you recite "Monday." I've always wondered how that thing goes. You're right. I am forty-five.

Eric, I didn't like some of the poetry I read either when I was your age. You may have to do what I did: write your own poems to get even. Serves them right, I say.

Joe, you are right. I am thirty-four. I'm also five feet eleven.

Amber, I'm glad you like poetry (unlike some people we won't mention). Yes, I have glasses, mostly for orange juice, although milk works in them too.

Kristen, I don't know how you did it. I am forty seven! And I do like to watch TV, but my wife won't let me turn it on so some nights I'm like really, really, totally bored.

Paul, yes, I am thirty-six. Please don't tell the others.

Laura, you must stop reading trash by that guy Silverstein and read only wonderful poems by me. Me. Me. Only me. For the rest of your life. Got that? Well, you might slip in a few thousand other good books, but just don't tell me about it.

TJ, I am tall, and I'm thirty, and I love pizza. You're amazing. Have you been peeking? Maybe my dog snitched. He's mad at me about having to sleep under the pillow.

Scott, if you like football better than poetry, we can still be friends. Maybe we ought to think up a poem about football. Did you see that long punt return against Denver Sunday? Now that was poetry in motion!

Garrick, there you go with that Silverstein guy again. You're as bad as Laura! Just for that I have a good notion not to tell you that you guessed my age correctly. You also got lucky on my height. I am six feet. Silverstein is two hundred years old, has no teeth, and is only three feet tall. Forget him.

Andy, you're way ahead of me. I only have one sister and one close friend. I also have one wife, one son, one daughter, one son-in-law, one daughter-in-law, and one dog. My one cat died. I wish I had learned to count higher when I was in school.

Kate, can you keep a secret? I am twenty! I also have a birthday in March so we're practically the same age.

Kristy, yes, sadly, I am of middle-age and it has robbed me of my sense of humor. I've looked everywhere for it. My dog looks smug and I suspect him of having something to do with it.

Thank you all for writing to me. I am looking forward to seeing you in March. In the meantime, forget that guy Silversmitt and concentrate on reading something worthwhile.

Sincerely,

David Harrison

Poetry Field Trip

Deborah Wooten, Fifth-Grade Teacher, Glenwood Landing School, Glen Head, NY

My students like some of the classical, traditional poets—maybe because I like them myself. When we were studying the Civil War, I read from the works of the Civil War poet, Walt Whitman. We read "O Captain! My Captain!" so many times they all knew it by heart; one person would start saying "O Captain! my Captain! our fearful trip is done," and the entire group would join in to complete the poem. I was happy when I found that Whitman had been born near our school; the family homestead had been turned into a county park. We went to see the site of Whitman's origins for ourselves; we read *Leaves of Grass* before and after the trip and learned that Whitman started a new kind of poetry—free verse. Those students will never forget Walt Whitman or his poetry. When they grow up they will take their kids to his birthplace and recite his poetry to them. The experience made a lasting impression on them.

TURN STUDENTS INTO WORD COLLECTORS

Help your students to become wordstruck. Create a graffiti wall.

A graffiti wall is a place to post interesting words and phrases for all poets to see. Brainstorm with students, do a word search for interesting words or phrases. You and the students can write words in black marker on strips of paper. Post the word strips on the bulletin board graffiti wall.

Grafitti walls are a good place to make the appeal of interesting words public but students need a private place to jot down words too. Encourage students to carry poetry notebooks with them at all times. Within these journals they can copy poems they like, record phrases and words that strike them, and germinate ideas for poems.

I Wonder, I Wish, I Remember Charts

Joie Hinden, High School English Teacher, Manhasset, NY

I have my students prepare a palette of words the same way a painter organizes colors, brushes, and canvases. They choose a topic to write about but before they begin to write, they list all the words and images they can think of related to that topic. Sometimes as a class or with a partner, we brainstorm for words to enrich their topic. I draw a chart of "I wonder," "I wish," and "I remember" statements, and they fill it in. They search for a paradox, a comparison, a contrast. They search for

Let <u>said</u> go to bed	Put <u>nice</u> on ice	Take the talk out of <u>walk</u>
mumbled	appealing	scuttled
stuttered	hot	sauntered
gasped	engaging	scrabbled
	zowie	

words that snap, crackle, pop (onomatopoeia). They collect substitutes, or synonyms, for common words such as *said*. As a group we create charts. They write more fluidly when they have a resource like a poetry palette at hand. Brainstorming generates new ideas; they think more freely, make new associations, and think in ways they had not thought before.

Read the Walls

1. Fill the walls with poetry (call-response chants, poem of the week, curriculum-based poems).

2. Give students the activity choice of reading the walls (they go around and read).

3. Create a time line on a clothes line across one side of the room. Put poets on the time line.

4. Display student work.

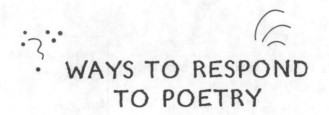

WAYS TO RESPOND TO POETRY

Using a Reader Response Technique

Nance S. Wilson, Sixth Grade Teacher, Lake Highland Preparatory School, Orlando, FL

Literary criticism of poetry is a complex skill, yet one children can accomplish. I use a reader response technique that helps children to personally respond to simple as well as sophisticated poems. I read aloud the poem two or three times. Then I display prompts on the overhead, such as:

1. How did the poem make you feel?

2. Did the poem make you see something in a different way? Explain.

3. Tell me a part of the poem that you liked/disliked and why.

4. Which words helped you to see pictures in your mind? (fantastic phrases)

5. What part of the poem surprised you?

Students respond to the prompts in writing and then share them in small groups. After a few minutes, they share their responses with the entire class. This technique garners complex insights from students, perhaps because they have a choice of entry points into interpreting the poem. It's less threatening than when a teacher says, "What does this poem mean?"

Easy Poetry Lessons That Dazzle and Delight ● Scholastic Professional Books

Post Fantastic Phrases

Sandra Brand, Fourth-Grade Teacher,
Academy School, Madison, CT

Every time I read poetry out loud, students hold
their poetry notebooks and two students work
at an easel with big chart paper. They write
down any "Fantastic Phrases" they hear. In our
search for what I like to call "Fantastic Phrases"
we list all kinds of pearls. Poets are especially
strong at stringing phrases into metaphors and similes. I think similes are
the easier of the two to teach. Once the kids understand that *like* and *as* are
the clues a literary detective uses to locate similes, then they can understand
that metaphor is a sister or brother to simile without the *like* or *as*.

Have students look for fantastic phrases in novels, picture books,
newspapers, advertisements, and comic strips.

Use Poetry Writing to Teach Syntax, Tone, and Diction

Carol Croland, Fourth-Grade Teacher, Echo Horizon School,
Los Angeles, CA

On a weekly basis, students first read poetry by adult poets such as
William Carlos Williams, Wallace Stevens, or William Blake before beginning a poem of their own. They are encouraged to discover the meaning
of their poems through the process of writing them. By approaching poetry writing in this way, a sense of wonder and excitement is connected to
the writing process. In writing poems, students have the opportunity to
playfully explore elements of language such as syntax, tone, and diction.
Writing poetry also increases students' understanding of a wide range of
concepts studied in language arts; for instance, writing a poem about a
color is a way for students to explore the purpose and use of adjectives.
Poetry writing has helped many students conquer a fear of writing. The
fear is gone, and they are developing a love, understanding, and apprecia-
tion not only for poetry writing, but more saliently, for writing in general!

Read Aloud Poetry in the Press

Marci Vogel, Sixth-Grade Teacher, Echo Horizon School, Culver City, CA
The Book Review Section of the local newspaper prints poetry every
Sunday, and sometimes there's a poem in there that I think the kids will

really like. Each student receives a copy and everyone sits in a circle on the floor. We read it aloud and share comments or ideas about the selection. (I've tried having the kids read, but the rhythm of a poem isn't always easy to achieve. When I read, I can usually convey some of the meaning.) The kids love the idea that I think they're ready to talk about "adult poetry," and they usually demonstrate a good sense of the poem's meaning, even if they can't always articulate it exactly. It seems that, just by giving the students a chance, letting them know that YOU think they can handle a "difficult" text, they will, in turn, take chances in their reading and in their responses. This sense of freedom leads to some amazing insights. Or maybe it's just that they get to lie down on the rug and relax for a while.

Use Sticky-notes to Chart Responses

Deborah Wooten, Fifth-Grade Teacher Glenwood Landing School, Glen Head, NY

One week I read "The King's Day" by Aliki. It is about King Louis XIV, who called himself the Sun King. I also read the poem "The Eclipse" by Jacques Prevert. At first students did not catch the joke about the eclipse of the Sun King. As they wrote and talked, they made the connection. Here are the steps I take.

1. Read aloud a poem or collection of poems or a story related to poems.
2. Ask students to reflect on a way they can connect to something in the poems.
3. Have students write their connections on sticky-notes.
4. Ask students to read their connections aloud individually, one at a time.
5. Place each written connection on a large chart with the date and title of the book written at the top. Label categories and develop new ones as the need arises. Sample categories include: literature, history, family, media, personal, time line, science, math. If we need a new category, we think of a good name for it and make it up.

Fall in Love with a Poem

Brod Bagert, Poet, New Orleans, LA

Teach children poetry to help them become poetry lovers. No generation has so desperately needed to hear the voice of poetry, and that voice will be the gift of the elementary classroom teacher. What is a poetry lover? A poetry lover is a person who loves at least one poem. Children may study

Steps in Performing Poetry

1. Teacher models—either reading or reciting a poem.

2. Invite students to try one line as a group.

3. Try one line with a partner, individually.

4. Students work in little teams/groups to practice.

5. Present to group.

poetry and they may write it, but they need to do neither to be poetry lovers. The world is full of music lovers who have never studied or composed music. The same is true for poetry.

Children find the poems they love in the same way they find the music they love—they hear it. We cannot fully experience music by looking at it with our eyes, we must hear it with our ears. A poem blossoms when the words are read aloud, and not just read but performed. First the teacher performs, establishing the model, then the children perform. When the voice of a poem and the identity of a child merge in dramatic performance, it is the beginning of a lifelong relationship.

Display children's poetry throughout the year.

Poetry Booklists

POETIC PICTUREBOOKS

Fox, Mem. *Wilfrid Gordon McDonald Partridge*. Illustrated by Julie Vivas. Kane/Miller. 1985.

Harrison, David. *The Animals' Song*. Illustrated by Chris L. Demarest. Boyds Mills Press, 1997.

Harrison, David. *When The Cows Come Home*. Illustrated by Chris L. Demarest. Boyds Mills Press, 1994.

Rylant, Cynthia. *The Relatives Came*. Illustrated by Stephen Gammell. Bradbury, 1985.

Rylant, Cynthia. *All I See*. Illustrated by Peter Catalanotto. Orchard, 1988.

Thomas, Joyce Carol. *Brown Honey in Broomwheat Tea*. Illustrated by Floyd Cooper. HarperCollins, 1993.

Willard, Nancy. *A Visit to William Blake's Inn: Poems for Innocent and Experienced Travelers*. Illustrated by Alice and Martin Provensen. Harcourt Brace, 1981.

STORY POEMS (NARRATIVE POEMS)

Longfellow, Henry Wadsworth. *Paul Revere's Ride*. Illustrated by Ted Rand. Dutton, 1990.

Poe, Edgar Allen. *Annabel Lee*. Illustrated by Gilles Tibo. Tundra, 1987.

Thayer, Ernest L. *Casey at the Bat*. Illustrated by Wallace Tripp. Putnam, 1888; 1989.

CONCRETE POEMS

Froman, Robert. *Seeing Things: A Book of Poems*. Lettering by Ray Barber. HarperCollins, o.p.

Lewis, J. Patrick. *Doodle Dandies: Poems That Take Shape*. Images by Lisa Desimini. Atheneum, 1998.

Livingston, Myra Cohn. *O Sliver of Liver and Other Poems*. Illustrated by Iris Van Rynbach. Atheneum, 1979.

LIMERICKS AND RIDDLES

Lear, Edward. *Daffy Down Dillies: Silly Limericks*. Illustrated by John O'Brien. Boyds Mills Press, 1992.

Lear, Edward. *The Owl and the Pussy-cat and Other Nonsense Poems*. (Illustrated and selected by Michael Hague). North-South Books, 1995.

Lewis, J. Patrick. *Riddle-Lightful: Oodles of Little Riddle Poems*. Illustrated by Debbie Tilley. Knopf, 1998.

Livingston, Myra Cohn (selected by). *Lots of Limericks*. Illustrated by Rebecca Perry. McElderry, 1991.

FREE VERSE

Adoff, Arnold. *Slow Dance Heart Break Blues*. Illustrated by William Cotton. Lothrop, 1995.

Harrison, David. *The Purchase of Small Secrets*. Illustrated by Karen Dugan and Meryl Henderson. Boyds Mills Press, 1998.

Herrera, Juan Felipe. *Laughing Out Loud, I Fly: Poems in English and Spanish*. Illustrated by Karen Barbour. HarperCollins, 1998.

Hopkins, Lee Bennett. *Been to Yesterdays: Poem of a Life*. Illustrated by Charlene Rendeiro. Wordsong/Boyds Mills Press, 1995.

Soto, Gary. *Neighborhood Odes*. Illustrated by David Diaz. Harcourt Brace, 1992.

BALLADS AND SONNETS

Child, Lydia Marie. *Over the River and Through the Wood*. Illustrated by Iris Van Rynbach. Little, Brown, 1989.

Livingston, Myra Cohn. *Let Freedom Ring: A Ballad of Martin Luther King, Jr.* Illustrated by Samuel Byrd. Holiday, 1992.

Spier, Peter (Illustrator). *The Star Spangled Banner*. Doubleday, 1973.

ANTHOLOGIES

Goldstein, Bobbye S. (Selected by). *Inner Chimes: Poems on Poetry*. Illustrated by Jane Breskin Zalben. Boyds Mills Press, 1992.

Kennedy, X.J. and Dorothy M. Kennedy (selected by). *Talking Like the Rain: A Read-to-Me Book of Poems*. Illustrated by Jane Dyer. Little, Brown, 1992.

Koch, Kenneth and Kate Farrell (selected and introduced by). *Talking to the Sun: An Illustrated Anthology of Poems for Young People*. Metropolitan Museum of Art/Henry Holt, 1985.

Rosen, Michael (selected by). *Classic Poetry: An Illustrated Collection*. Illustrated by Paul Howard. Candlewick, 1998.

Untermeyer, Louis (Selected and with commentary by). *The Golden Books Family Treasury of Poetry*. New introduction by Leonard S. Marcus. Illustrated by Joan Walsh Anglund. Golden Books, 1998.

SELECTED BOOKS BY DAVID HARRISON

Somebody Catch My Homework. Illustrated by Betsy Lewin. Boyds Mills Press, 1993.

The Boy Who Counted Stars. Illustrated by Betsy Lewin. Boyds Mills Press, 1994.

A Thousand Cousins: Poems of Family Life. Illustrated by Betsy Lewin. Boyds Mills Press, 1996.

The Book of Giant Stories. McGraw-Hill, 1972.

RESOURCES FOR THE TEACHER

Benton, Michael, J. Teasey, R. Bell, E. K. Hurst. *Young Readers Responding to Poems*. Routledge, 1988.

Chatton. Barbara. *Using Poetry Across the Curriculum.* Oryx 1993.

Cullinan, Bernice E., Marilyn Scala, Virginia Schroder. *Three Voices: An Invitation to Poetry Across the Curriculum.* Teachers Pub Group, 1995.

Hopkins, Lee Bennett. *Pass the Poetry Please.* 23rd edition, HarperCollins, 1998.

Hulme, Joy N. and Donna W. Guthrie. *How to Write, Recite, Delight in All Kinds of Poetry.* Millbrook, 1996.

Janeczco, Paul B. *Favorite Poetry Lessons.* Scholastic Professional Books, 1998.

Larrick, Nancy. *Let's Do a Poem*! Delacorte, 1991.

Livingston, Myra Cohn. *Climb Into the Bell Tower: Essays on Poetry.* HarperCollins, 1990.

Livingston, Myra Cohn. *Poem Making: Ways to Begin Writing Poetry.* HarperCollins, 1991.

McVitty, Walter (Ed.). *Word Magic: Poetry as a Shared Adventure.* Primary English Teaching Association, Australia, 1985.

Steinbergh, Judith. *Reading and Writing Poetry.* Scholastic Professional Books, 1994.

Sweeney, Jacqueline. *Teaching Poetry: Yes You Can!.* Scholastic Professional Books, 1993.

MORE OF OUR FAVORITES

Dotlich, Rebecca Kai. *Lemonade Sun.* Illustrated by Jan Spivey Gilchrist. Wordsong/Boyds Mills Press, 1998.

Fletcher, Ralph. *Relatively Speaking: Poems about Family.* Illustrated by Walter Lyon Krudop. Orchard Books, 1999.

Florian, Douglas. *Laugh-eteria: Poems and Drawings.* Harcourt Brace, 1999.

George, Kristine O'Connell. *Old Elm Speaks; Tree Poems.* Illustrated by Kate Kiesler. Clarion, 1998.

Gunning, Monica. *Not a Copper Penny in Me House: Poems from the Caribbean.* Illustrated by Frane' Lessac. Wordsong/Boyds Mills Press, 1993.

Hopkins, Lee Bennett. *Hand in Hand: American History Through Poetry.* Illustrated by Peter M. Fiore. Simon & Schuster, 1994.

Kuskin, Karla. *The Upstairs Cat.* Illustrated by Howard Fine. Clarion, 1997.

Schertle, Alice. *A Lucky Thing: Poems by Alice Schertle.* Illustrated by Wendell Minor. Harcourt Brace, 1999.

Strickland, Michael (editor). *My Own Song and Other Poems to Groove To.* Illustrated by Eric Sabee. Wordsong/ Boyds Mills Press, 1997.

CHAPTER 2:
What Poetry Is All About

Josh's letter came from Valparaiso, Indiana. Nelda Silva had just read a book of poetry to her third graders, and Josh wanted me to know why he liked a poem of mine about a naughty boy, "Bobby Gene McQuig."

"I like it because it's funny," he began. "It reminds me of my brother, Joseph. And some of my friends at school. And a movie I saw called *Dennis the Menace*. And it reminds me of the Three Stooges, named Larry, Curly, and Moe."

Josh got a lot of mileage from one poem. When his teacher read the poem aloud, the words stimulated Josh to make associations and create mind pictures of his own. As a third grader, Josh might have had a hard time explaining what poetry is all about, but he demonstrated it beautifully. Poetry is about words, and it's about associations. How we put our words together helps us share our mind pictures with the reader. But it also stimulates the reader to personalize the poem by imagining his own associations.

Something about my class showoff made Josh think about his family (brother), school (friends), Dennis the Menace, and some slapstick comics who performed years before he was born. Such strong associations help us develop feelings of ownership about favorite poems. Maybe that's why we say, "My favorite poem," rather than, "Your poem that I like best."

So how do we put our words together to make a poem? Where do we begin? The good news is that everyone is a poet, and that's especially true of children. Their world is constructed of associations and metaphors where horses fly, scarecrows talk, and spiders write life-saving messages. Even a fifth grader's obligatory thank-you note can turn into poetry.

> *I haven't got much time.*
> *I've got other things to do.*
> *You took your time to tell us about your books,*
> *So I'll just say, "Thank you!"*
> *Ramin Herati*
> *Ms. (Jennifer) Jackson's Class*

Ramin may not have known that he had just composed a quatrain (verse with four lines) called a short ballad. It wasn't necessary to know the technical terms to express himself. He had a need ("Today we'll write the nice man who visited our class. Get out your paper.") and an idea ("I'll keep this short and clever"). He chose words that suited his purpose and got on with the task at hand.

We want to help kids choose what works for them and get on with writing poetry. We'll introduce terms and guidelines, but the strategies are designed to excite young poets. Everyone can create pictures in the mind and stimulate associations. That's the essence of poetry. That's what it's all about.

STRATEGY 1:
IMAGERY

Background

Artists use colors and brushes to paint pictures of the world they see. Poets use words. Equipped with a pencil, an imagination, and the right words, they create pictures in the mind for their readers. What we like best about our favorite poems may be that we "see" and "feel" what they mean. We understand how funny they are, or sad, or quiet because the poets have given us fresh pictures to think about. Their imagery shows us something familiar in a new way. Encourage students to think in terms of all five senses when creating images for their poems. Ask questions that stimulate their imaginations, and students jump right in. Let's say you're describing snow. You might ask, What is it like? What is it colder than? Whiter than? As soft as? As silent as? What does it taste like? How does it feel? What does it mean? School closed? Snowmen? Snowball fights?

Encourage students to think of snow as something else. Snow is ice cream. Frozen fingers. Snow angels. Frosty breath. Jingle bells. Christmas. Gift giving. Cards. Or, if you live in an area where there is no snow, snow is a picture. It's Christmas carols. It's a spray can.

Two-Minute Warm-up

Start five columns at the top of the blackboard: Sound, Taste, Smell, Touch, and Sight. Ask students to offer sensory-rich subjects that spring to mind, and list these. For example, in the sound column, *crickets*; under taste, *fried chicken*; smell, *leaves burning*; touch, *mud*; sight, *a moonlit lake*.

Activity

Have each student choose an image from the columns and write a paragraph or so of details about the image. Encourage students to involve sensory details. What do you see? What color is it? What sounds do you hear? What do they remind you of? What do you smell? What do you

OTHER IMAGERY-RICH POETS TO TRY

. . . .

1. Jane Yolen, *Snow, Snow* (Boyds Mills Press, 1998)

2. Barbara Juster Esbensen, *Words With Wrinkled Knees* (Boyds Mills Press, 1998)

3. Rebecca Kai Dotlich, *Lemonade Sun* (Boyds Mills Press, 1998)

4. Valerie Worth, *All the Small Poems and Fourteen More* (Farrar, Straus, & Giroux, 1994)

5. Kristine O'Connell George, *The Great Frog Race and Other Poems,* (Houghton Mifflin, 1997)

taste? What can you touch? Students can build these images into a poem. For now, form is not important. Just remind them that poems are composed of lines and stanzas as opposed to sentences and paragraphs. The lines can be long or short. Students can use punctuation or not.

TEACHING TIP

Give students photocopies of the poems on pages 29 and 30. Read the poems aloud, and ask the students to share their favorite images. What kind of images are they (sight? sound? touch?)? How are the two poems different? Let the students discover that one poem uses rhymes while the other doesn't. Is there a reason the poet writing about the sea might choose to use rhyming words? The repetition of the rhyming sounds echoes the rhythm of the tide (the breathing of the sea) as it washes onto the shore. Have the students underline other sounds that repeat. For example, in the first line, *saw* and *sea*; later, *wind* and *water*. "Looking Down in the Rain" isn't so much about movement and relies more on surprising visual images.

Which poem do they like better? Why?

Looking Down in the Rain

In the big puddle
at the bus stop
I see the city standing
on its head.

Tops of buildings
move under my boots.
A wavery red light
wiggles
to green.

The school bus
orange as a pumpkin
wobbles in on its roof
and stops.
In the puddle
I see small faces
and yellow leaves swimming
under water!

—Barbara Juster Esbensen

Until I Saw the Sea

Until I saw the sea
I did not know
that wind
could wrinkle water so.

I never knew
that sun
could splinter a whole sea of blue.

Nor
did I know before,
a sea breathes in and out
upon a shore.

—Lilian Moore

Easy Poetry Lessons That Dazzle and Delight ● Scholastic Professional Books

STRATEGY 2:
GROUP POEMS

Background

A poet working alone doesn't have the advantage of 25 other imaginations. Creating collaborative poems involves everyone in the process of thinking about the same idea, so it's a good way to get children started with poetry writing.

Read aloud the group poem "On the Playground" on page 32 and ask students to respond to it. Point out that many sound images are grouped in the first half and that later lines involve the senses of sight and touch.

Two-Minute Warm-up

Have students suggest busy events, places, or occasions that all of them have attended. As a class, choose one place or activity to write a group poem about.

Activity

Ask students to suggest every observation and description they can think of surrounding your chosen topic as you list them on the blackboard. Notice which categories the suggestions fall into and group them accordingly. For example, after three descriptions of sounds, you can designate an area on the board for "sounds" and ask specifically if there are other suggestions for that category. What smells are there? How is the place decorated? Is it hot, is it cold? What are people doing there? What kind of people are they? When you have plenty of suggestions, start organizing the material into a poem. What is the first thing you want a reader to experience about this place? Do you want to present this poem in a time sequence (from beginning to end of an event) or should the focus of the poem move from place to place? Not all of the suggested material will fit in this one poem. Be selective about what you keep.

When the class has agreed on a general sequence, start at the beginning of the poem and discuss how the observations and descriptions might be improved by images such as those discussed in Strategy 1.

On the Playground (A group poem)

I hear the basketball bouncing on the court,

and kids shouting,

and the jump rope swishing and slapping the ground,

     and the click-clack of feet.

     "Click clack, paddy wack…"

     "Teddy bear, teddy bear, turn around."

The birds are chirping,

the wind is whistling,

the rocks are crumbling,

leaves are rustling.

Kids are skidding on the stones,

stopping.

We find caterpillars,

     they look like rugs

     and feel soft as silk.

     They tickle your arm.

Inch worms are hanging from trees

     like green rain.

You can smell the flowers.

When children pick up buttercups,

     they press yellow egg on their arms

     and learn if they love butter.

The whistle blows!

"Time to go in!"

       —Mary Dunn's first grade, Heath School

       facilitated by Judith Steinbergh

    Easy Poetry Lessons That Dazzle and Delight ● Scholastic Professional Books

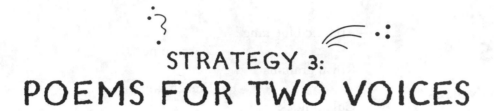

STRATEGY 3:
POEMS FOR TWO VOICES

Background

Sometimes the best way to say what we want is to have more than one voice speaking. An example is "Fishes," Georgia Heard's poem for two voices on the next page. Before you read it aloud, pretend you are swimming in the ocean on a fine, clear day. A brightly colored fish appears and looks you in the eye. Another comes, then another until the water is filled with schools of exotic fishes. They begin to introduce themselves! "We are fishes," says first one group then another. If you write a poem about such an encounter, you may need to tell it with two voices. Although the voices don't speak directly to one another, the poet can alternate voices or have them speak at the same time.

Two-Minute Warm-up

How many other ideas for two voices can your students think of? Here are some to help them begin. Swinging/Swings Creaking. Inside Recess/Sound of Raining. Going to Feed the Dogs/Dogs Barking Hungrily. Doing homework/T.V. blaring. Two family members thinking out loud or talking.

Activity

Working with a partner, each student can write one voice of a poem for two voices. Ask them to balance their poem so that each voice is heard about equally. **Hint:** It's all right if sometimes both voices "speak" at the same time. It also works to have the second voice as an echo of the first, a technique used in Paul Fleishman's book *Joyful Noise* (HarperCollins, 1988).

Fishes

Poem for two voices

Atlantic blue tang	
	Zebra pipe
Royal gramma	
	French angel
Cuban hock	
	Golden butterfly
We	We
are	are
fishes	fishes
We	We
shimmer	swim
under	
	water
Our	Our
mouths	mouths
open	
and	
	close
Our	Our
gills	gills
sift	
air	
	from
	water
Our	Our
fins	fins
steer	
us	
	like
	wings
We	We
are	are
fishes	fishes
We	We
shimmer	swim

—Georgia Heard

STRATEGY 4:
DIALOGUE POEMS

Background

Once at a school I visited the playground at recess. A little boy and a little girl, standing nose-to-nose, were taking turns screaming at each other. "Yowww!" he'd yell and she, giggling, would practically fall over backward. Then she'd square her shoulders, fill her lungs, and shriek, "Eiiii!" and he would crumple with laughter. Maybe that's how cave people sounded in their first conversations.

People talking (or yelling!) can make interesting poems. On the next page read aloud "Talking to the Horse Trainer" by Nancy Springer. It's a conversation between a young girl and the horse trainer.

Two-Minute Warm-up

A dialogue poem is a conversation between two different voices. Dialogue poems can help us express all sorts of relationships. How about Parent/Child? Bus driver/Student. Clerk/Customer. Brother/Sister. Grandparent/Child. Two Strangers. Ask students to suggest all the relationships they can think of in a two-minute period and list them on the board.

Activity

Have pairs of students choose a relationship from the list and role-play it for five minutes. Next, have students write a page or so of conversation. On another sheet of paper, they can begin to select and arrange statements into a rough poem. If they choose to model their poem on "Talking to the Horse Trainer," encourage them to make the dialogue crisp. They can then choose another relationship and write a dialogue poem of their own. They might enjoy collaborating on a poem with a family member. A dialogue poem can use any form, so suggest that students try different formats.

> ### TEACHING TIP
> ....
>
> Not all dialogue poems are between two people. Inanimate objects can be given voices as well. The wind can talk to a river, the moon to the sun. A child can converse with a favorite doll or argue with a shoelace that refuses to stay tied. Invite students to imagine other possible conversations for poems. Remind them to listen to the sounds of the words they choose for various voices. A lazy cat's voice might sound different from the voice of a hyperactive chihuahua. The voice of the wind could actually contain or echo the sounds of wind.

Talking to the Horse Trainer

"You been kicked?"
   "Yep."
"Did it hurt?"
   "Yep."
"You been bitten?"
   "Yep."
"That hurt too?"
   "Uh-huh."
"Been run away with?"
   "Some days."
"Take a fall?"
   "Now and then."
"Get stepped on?"
   "Once."
"More than once."
   "That's true."
"How many times?"
   "Maybe twice."
"More than that."
   "What's your point?"
"Look at me."
   "Okay, I'm looking at you. So?"
"How come you still love horses?"
   "How come I still love you?"

—Nancy Springer

STRATEGY 5:
LIST POEMS

Background

List poems, like group poems, can involve everyone in the class. Poets pick a subject and make a list of ideas, objects, or actions about that subject. One of my list poems, "Our Little Brother," lists a little brother's 17 names, which is why it takes so long to call him to open the back door. "Whale Chant," by Georgia Heard, lists 12 kinds of whales swimming in the deep blue sea. Felice Holman wrote "The City Dump" in which she lists all the crusts and crumbs, pits of plums, white eggshells, and green-blue smells that one might find there. On the following page are two clever list poems by Dorothy Aldis and Mary O'Neill.

Two-Minute Warm-Up

List everything about school that you can think of in two minutes (home-work, friends, recess, cafeteria food, bullies, teachers, school nurse, etc.). If you prefer, choose a different subject such as family, camping out, a pet, or being sick.

Activity

Suggest beginning lines for each subject that help frame the poem. "You know you're camping when..." Work with the class to write at least one list poem together. Then ask students to write one of their own. Exchange the finished poems, and take turns reading them aloud.

Wasps

Wasps like coffee.
Syrup.
Tea.
Coca-Cola.
Butter.
Me.

—Dorothy Aldis

Sound of Water

The sound of water is:
Rain,
Lap,
Fold,
Slap,
Gurgle,
Splash,
Churn,
Crash,
Murmur,
Pour,
Ripple,
Roar,
Plunge,
Drip,
Spout,
Skip,
Sprinkle,
Flow,
Ice,
Snow.

—Mary O'Neill

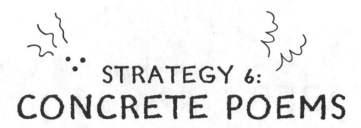

STRATEGY 6:
CONCRETE POEMS

Background

Just as some words mimic the sounds they stand for (onomatopoeia), some entire poems imitate the shapes of their subjects. We call such artistic creations concrete poems (or shaped or picture poems). Because they combine art with poetry, they may have special appeal to the visual learners among your students. Some concrete poems make simple pictures by adjusting the lengths of lines to create the general shape of a butterfly, say, or a bottle or a ball. More elablorate ones involve the size and shape of the lettering, the placement of letters and words on the page, and even the color of the ink or paper. The two poems by Robert Froman on page 40, are good examples of a visual poem.

Two-Minute Warm-up

Ask students to suggest objects or animals with distinctive shapes that might inspire them to write a poem. **Hint:** an anteater's nose, a python's body, a cat's back, a turtle's shell.

Activity

Show examples of concrete poems to your students. Also display books of graphic art, or the work of artists such as Vasily Kandinsky or Frank Stella. Children can study these resources to get ideas for their own concrete poems. Concrete poetry is contagious—children will want to create their own. Give them materials—markers, paints, computer graphics, collage materials to work with. Ask each student to create a concrete poem and exhibit the results on your "concrete" wall.

DIS
RE APPEARER

Duck on the water.
He's gone!
Where?
Oh.

Diving

duck.

again.

comes

Here he

WHEE

PACKED SNOW STEEP HILL FAST SLED

—Robert Froman

STRATEGY 7:
NARRATIVE POEMS

Background

Poets generally create pictures for the mind by drawing our attention to one or a few details such as a purple cow or the yard white with new snow. But with narrative poems, we get a whole story. Just as concrete poems combine poetry with art, narrative poems combine poetry with storytelling. In writing "A Brief Romance" (next page), I wanted to build suspense toward the "inevitable" disaster, when the hen allowed the fox in, and I wanted a surprise ending. Nearly everyone likes a good story, but it may come as a surprise to some that many of the best stories are also poems.

Two-Minute Warm-up

Bring in a photograph of you with someone in your family. Show it to the class and then tell a favorite story about you and that person, or simply describe where you were when the photo was taken.

Activity

As the warm-up demonstrated, most of us have a favorite story—about ourselves, a family member, or an escapade with a friend. Invite students to bring in a snapshot from home and share the story behind it with a partner, who can ask questions that clarify the details. Then students can turn these oral stories into poems. Take turns reading the poems aloud, and discuss how these narrative poems tell their stories.

A Brief Romance

"Oh Mistress Hen,
Won't you let me in?"
The fox asked
With a foxy grin,
But the hen said, "I'm too clever."

"I love you so,"
He murmured low,
"Just one little squeeze,
And then I'll go,"
But the hen just cackled, "Never!"

"Don't make me blue,
My sweet Baboo,
I'd do anything
For you,"
But the hen said, "No you wouldn't."

"My knees are weak,
I can scarcely speak,
I long to kiss
Your lovely beak,"
And the hen said, "I just coudn't."

He winked and he smiled,
"My darling child,
I'll only stay
A little while,"
And the hen said, "We really shouldn't."

At last the hen
Let the fox come in,
And no one knows
What happened then,
Though it only took a minute.

I can only say,
When she hopped away,
Her tummy was round
And it made her sway,
And I think the fox was in it.

—David Harrison

STRATEGY 8:
SIMILE

Background

Similes help us understand one thing by comparing it with another. We use similes when we say he runs *like* a deer or those clouds look *like* cottage cheese. To take a risk is *like* tickling a dragon. In "Conversation," Lisa Bahlinger describes the sudden blossoming of sunflowers: "...today they burst open like music." Monica Gunning's Nana, in "Walking To Church," carries "...her Sunday shoes like a treasure." Marie Louise Allen's snow covered bushes (next page) look "like popcorn-balls," and Rachel Field's thoughts are "as thick as fireflies."

Two-Minute Warm-up

Have students picture a cat cuddled up and purring next to them on a couch. Ask, what does it sound like? (*a motor, a bullfrog*) What does the curled cat remind you of? (*a crescent roll, a sleeping baby*). Now read aloud the following list of simile jumpstarts, and invite students to share whatever comes to mind.

> *The full moon is like...*
> *A bubbling brook sounds like...*
> *The cafeteria at lunch time is like ...*
> *Falling asleep is like...*
> *Red sounds like...*
> *Yellow tastes like...*
> *Anger is like...*

Activity

Have each student choose a subject, brainstorm similes for it, then write a poem using this image bank. As they start to shape their poems, ask questions such as, Which simile interests you most? Which is the most unusual? Which seems truest?

First Snow

Snow makes whiteness where it falls.

The bushes look like popcorn-balls.

And places where I always play,

Look like somewhere else today.

—Marie Louise Allen

Some People

Isn't it strange some people make

    You feel so tired inside,

Your thoughts begin to shrivel up

    Like leaves all brown and dried!

But when you're with some other ones,

    It's stranger still to find

Your thoughts as thick as fireflies

    All shiny in your mind!

—Rachel Field

STRATEGY 9:
METAPHOR

Background

A simile may compare one thing with another, but compared to a metaphor, it's like a wimp. A metaphor doesn't mess around. It just comes right out and says what it means. You're not *like* a toad; you *are* a toad! He's a turkey. She's my whole world. My toes are ice. My dog's a pussycat and my cat's a tiger. Turning one thing into something else helps us understand how a poet feels about the subject. Look for the metaphors in the next two poems. Eve Merriam extended one metaphor throughout her poem, while I moved from one metaphor to another in the second stanza.

Two-Minute Warm-up

Look around the room with your students. Using metaphors, turn everything you see into something else: chalkboard (mirror for teacher's thoughts), desks (perches), windows (the building's eyes), rows of chairs (train cars), artwork (polka-dotted walls), kids (all tongues and feet). To give the activity further focus, compare objects in your classroom to animals.

Activity

Ask students, working individually, to use metaphors in poems about some other location, such as the dentist's office, the mall, or a pet store. Have them try to extend the metaphor throughout the poem, and point out that this requires they stay on one train of thought. For example, if sitting in the dentist chair getting a cavity filled is being compared to a construction site, then the drill is a jackhammer, the teeth are concrete blocks, the filling is mortar, and so on.

Metaphor

Morning is
a new sheet of paper
for you to write on.

Whatever you want to say,
all day,
until night
folds it up
and files it away.

The bright words and the dark words
are gone
until dawn
and a new day
to write on.

—Eve Merriam

Clucking Away the Day

Banana cream pie clouds
baking in the sun,
last tasty morsels
melting in the blue.

Chewing grass, I watch,
content as a hen on her nest,
clucking away the day.

—David Harrison

CHAPTER 3:
Playing With Words

I had a teacher who loved words. He had a way of lingering over his favorites, touching them lovingly with his tongue, tasting them like chocolate drops. When he pronounced window sill, "winn-dow silll," we could hear the wind blowing through the word. The lowly marshmallow, offered as "marrsh-melll-o," sounded like an exotic treat for kings. Our class plotted ways to get him to read to us.

Playing with words must be an ancient game. I imagine a clan of ancestors, huddled uneasily around their cave fire. They gaze into an angry, rain-sodden night exploding with sky-splitting spears, crashes that widen the eyes and jar limestone walls, and shrieking winds that snap tree limbs like bird bones. Early efforts to recount such a night must have been filled with guttural approximations of the natural sounds they heard.

Children learn to speak by approximating the sounds they hear, and they entertain themselves by playing with those sounds. Poetry is an extension of that play. We have invented some rules to play by—length, number, and arrangement of lines, patterns of accents, rhyme schemes, and such—but the words themselves often hold the key to successful poems.

Think of the ways in which we describe fire. It roars. It hisses. It sizzles. It snaps and crackles and pops. Fire, in short, is a very busy word. Water, on the other hand, is a noun of many moods. Oh, it roars and pounds and crashes. But it can also crawl (according to Tennyson), roll (Old Man River), trickle, babble, and soothe.

This chapter presents ways for students to play and experiment with words. They will learn that onomatopoeia words sound like what they stand for. Such words alone rarely make a good poem, but good poems often have such words in them.

Most kids may have heard about Peter Piper, who picked a peck of pickled peppers. Now they'll learn about alliterations and how to put them to work in their own poems.

Maybe you've read to your class Emily Dickinson's wonderful poem, "I'm Nobody! Who Are You?" One of Dickinson's special talents as a poet is the way she matches words that don't seem to rhyme, except somehow they go together (because they have vowels that *do* rhyme). That's called assonance, and we'll have a strategy about it.

In another lesson we will introduce the notion that the letters of words can be *physically* arranged—stretched out like giraffes, crammed together like birds in a nest—to help us make a point.

We play with long words and short ones in Elizabeth Coatsworth's "Sea Gull"—the short words are contained in the urgent warning: "Get down into the water, fish!"

Pooh Bear thinks up words to make his songs more "hummy," so we do too. Then we conclude with a strategy about the way words, when strung together just so, create special movements and rhythms that must be read aloud to be appreciated.

All in all, this is a playful chapter that offers words as a hearty diet. No low-cal stuff here. We invite kids to roll their words around, taste their delicious qualities, and hunger for more.

Easy Poetry Lessons That Dazzle and Delight ● Scholastic Professional Books

STRATEGY 10:
ONOMATOPOEIA

Background

Break a stick for firewood, it *snaps*. Rain on a campfire *hisses,* and thunder *rumbles*. Words that sound like what they mean are called *onomatopoeia*. Onomatopoeia words are fun to say; they add music to a poem. They're so expressive, some believe that they were the basis of human language. In Valerie Worth's poem "bell" on the next page, the first stanza includes the words *tink, tong, clang*, and *bong* in describing the sounds of a bell. The second stanza uses a metaphor ("The bell gives metal a tongue to sing") plus two other poetic devices—*alliteration* and *assonance*—which we'll talk about in the next two strategies.

Two-Minute Warm-up

Read aloud the poem "bell" and let the students discover what onomatopoeia is by discussing what the underlined words have in common. Have kids offer other onomatopoeia words. Make a list on chart paper (*rip, pop, sizzle, whoosh)*. When they run out of suggestions, make some noises in the classroom—close a door, open the window, drop some coins, write on the chalk board, spin a globe, pour a glass of water—and ask students to come up with words to describe the sounds they hear. If they can't think of any words, then have them make up words that sound like the action. After all, what's a word for the sound of brushing your teeth? (*shooga, shooga, shooga?)*

Activity

Select some of the words on the class list and have students share images that relate to the sound. Keep the list on display and invite children to use it to inspire their own onomatopoeic poems.

RIP
pants ripping, ripping open a bag of chips, ripping a piece of paper

POP
balloon popping, cork out of bottle

SIZZLE
butter in a frying pan

WHOOSH
the sound of a vacuum-packed jar of peanuts being opened, someone speeding close by you on a bicycle, a gust of wind blowing open the front door

bell

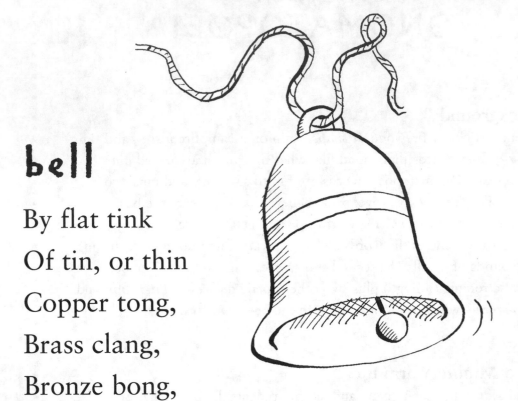

By flat tink
Of tin, or thin
Copper tong,
Brass clang,
Bronze bong,

The bell gives
Metal a tongue —
To sing
In one sound
Its whole song.

—Valerie Worth

Easy Poetry Lessons That Dazzle and Delight ● Scholastic Professional Books

STRATEGY 11:
ALLITERATION

Background

The repetition of initial consonant sounds close enough together that we're aware of them is called *alliteration*, as in the ball bounced into the basement, or Katie caught a cold in the creek. Though you can easily work with that definition, technically, alliteration can be defined as when:

- the consonants just before the first accented vowels are the same (<u>sw</u>eep/<u>sw</u>allow);
- the vowels are not pronounced alike (sw<u>ee</u>p/sw<u>a</u>llow); and
- the consonants that follow the vowels are different: (swee<u>p</u>/swa<u>ll</u>ow).

Here are a few more examples of alliteration: lick/line; leap/lad; follow/furry/feet.

Consonance is like alliteration except that the consonants both before *and* after the dissimilar vowel sounds are the same. Examples: **truck/trick; trance/trounce**.) Tongue twisters are famous for their alliteration. As Karla Kuskin demonstrates in "The Meal," on page 53, alliteration is often used for the sheer fun of the music it brings to a poem. To read it aloud is to treat your teeth and tongue to a tango.

Two-Minute Warm-up

Ask your students what they notice about the words in "The Meal" to help them come up with a definition of alliteration. How about the name of the poet who wrote "The Meal"? Do any of your students have alliterative names? Can they think of any people or characters whose names are alliterations? (*Ronald Reagan, Sammy Sosa, Captain Kangaroo, Mickey Mouse, Bugs Bunny*)

Have a student say aloud a word, and then each classmate, in turn, think of an alliteration to go with it. When you've gone all they way around the room, begin another round with a new word!

Activity

Have your students practice alliteration with a three-word poem. Use a noun, a verb and an adverb, in that order, and list them vertically. The three words should begin with the same sound and should say something interesting about the topic, the first word. Though short, this pattern is not easy, so allow some time for thought. Here are some examples:

TOPIC:	cows	flowers	rabbits	Steven	Billy
WHAT IT DOES:	consider	fold	riot	studies	bowls
HOW IT DOES IT:	calmly	finally	reluctantly	steadily	badly

TEACHING TIP: SOUND EFFECTS

Make children aware that the sound of words—as well as their meaning—contributes to the poem's mood. These sounds don't have to be just at the beginning of words. Have each student write a brief description of a scene involving mostly hard or loud actions—a baseball breaks a window, a football player tackles, two automobiles collide. Now have each student write a brief description of a quiet scene with soft objects—a baby falls asleep, butterflies flit in a garden, a person walks in a snowfall at night.

Put two columns on the board: *Hard Sounds* and *Soft Sounds*. Go through the alphabet with your students, pronouncing aloud all the consonant sounds: Is it a hard sound? (d, k, t); Is it soft? (f, s, m, v) Don't forget *ch, qu, th,* and *sh*. (The letter "c" can be hard or soft, depending on pronunciation, but its different sounds can be accounted for by "k" and "s.") If some sounds don't fit in either category, put them in a separate miscellaneous column. (If some of the "miscellaneous" sounds have a similar quality that the students can name, create another column for them.)

Now have the students look at the first description they wrote about the loud scene. Do the words they have chosen contain many of the hard sounds as categorized on the board? If not, can they replace some of their words with words that mean the same thing but feature more of these hard sounds? (cracked, shatter, destroy, dent) How do these hard sounds add to the effect of the description? Try the same exercise with the quiet descriptions, using the softer consonant sounds.

The Meal

Timothy Tompkins had turnips and tea.

The turnips were tiny.

He ate at least three.

And then, for dessert, he had onions and ice.

He liked that so much

that he ordered it twice.

He had two cups of ketchup,

a prune, and a pickle.

"Delicious," said Timothy.

"Well worth a nickel."

He folded his napkin

and hastened to add,

"It's one of the loveliest breakfasts I've had."

—Karla Kuskin

STRATEGY 12:
ASSONANCE

Background

Consonance depends on different vowel sounds between similar consonants (truck/trick or trance/trounce) *Assonance* involves same or similar vowel sounds between different consonants: hit/will; disturb/bird; cat/sad. Read aloud the poems on pages 56 and 57. Then read them again, stressing the examples of assonance (also called *vowel rhyme*). Alliteration, consonance, and assonance describe the same effort, which is to place words and lines together in ways that stress similar qualities of sound. The blended and varied sounds of poetry are important reasons why we love it. Children constantly play with the sounds of words—in cheers and taunts and songs and chants. It may surprise them that some of their games have names.

TEACHING TIP: "POLLIWOGS"

This poem is a wonderful example of using assonance, not only for the pleasure of its sound but for the way it reinforces the subject of the poem. Polliwogs are "plump" and almost every word in this poem uses the sounds of 'o', 'u' or 'ou' to echo that roundness. The polliwogs' mouths are round (line 4) and so is the reader's mouth as he reads this poem aloud. Ask your students to notice vowel sounds that are repeated in the poem. What kind of words would your students use if they were writing a poem about a praying mantis? Have the class brainstorm a few words to describe him and his movement (*thin, skinny, twig, stick, tiptoe, linger, lean)*. Think of other subjects whose definite shapes could be emphasized with assonant words.

TEACHING TIP: "FIRST BIRD OF SPRING"

In revising this early draft, David Harrison changed some of the words to create the harmony of assonance—to hint at birds' mysterious harmony of nature.

First Bird of Spring

You've seen so much
since you've been away,
sing me a song.

Sing of the mountains
you crossed last fall
through starry nights
and ~~morning rains~~ *blazing dawns*

Of rivers, bayous,
~~fields of corn,~~ *checkerboard farms*
glistening silos,
pigeony barns,

Sing of lightning,
~~stormy seas,~~ *wind-tossed waves*
ships at anchor,
~~peaceful~~ *tranquil* days.

You've seen so much
it will take all spring.
Sing me a song.

Two-Minute Warm-up

List one-syllable words with long vowels on the board, such as <u>lake</u>, <u>side</u>, or <u>crow</u>, and work with your kids to form lists of assonant words.

lake — amaze, straight, game, cane

side — wide, like, mine, pipe

crow — load, mold, poke, torn.

Activity

Use words from the list to write a group poem. It can be brief. And feel free to change the form of the words—for example, instead of *poke* use *poking.* Maybe your poem will be about an amazing lake where cane grows straight and game roams free; maybe about a crow poking into moldy sacks of corn.

Polliwogs

Come see

What I found!

Chubby commas,

Mouths round,

Plump babies

Stubby as toes.

Polliwogs!

Tadpoles!

Come see

What I found!

Frogs-in-waiting —

Huddled in puddles,

Snuggled in mud.

—Kristine O'Connell George

Easy Poetry Lessons That Dazzle and Delight ● Scholastic Professional Books

First Bird of Spring

You've seen so much
since you've been away,
sing me a song.

Sing of the mountains
you crossed last <u>fall</u>
through starry nights
and blazing <u>dawns</u>,

Of rivers, bayous,
checkerboard <u>farms</u>,
glistening silos,
pigeony <u>barns</u>.

<u>Sing</u> of lightning,
<u>wind</u>-tossed waves,
<u>ships</u> at anchor,
tran<u>quil</u> days.

You've seen so much
it will take all spring.
Sing me a song.

—David Harrison

STRATEGY 13:
ARRANGING WORDS
TO SUPPORT MEANING

Background

Read Arnold Spilka's delightful poem on page 60, "The Turtle," straight through *without* the pauses. Does something seem missing? Maybe we wonder why the turtle would say, "I don't know why I bother." But read the poem again with those important pauses and breaks that de-lib-er-ate-ly... slow... us down... to tur-tle... speed, and we understand. We also "get" the urgency of "One Thing On My Mind" when we see the words jammed together, spilling out all at once in a desperate plea. (I was answering "questions" in a kindergarten class when a girl informed me emphatically she had to go to the bathroom. I wrote the poem the way she sounded.) When words aren't enough to get our message across, we arrange them to "show" what we mean with spacing.

TEACHING TIP

Just as the arrangement of words can affect tempo, so can the length of the words the poet chooses. A character moving across a room quickly can *skip, dash,* or *march.* A slower character might *saunter, shuffle or waddle.* These words not only describe a slower pace, they are two syllables long and take longer to say or read. The poet can further lengthen a word (and the time it takes the character to cross the room) by changing the form of the verb—*sauntering* or *waddling*—or can search for an even longer word like *meander* or *promenade.* Adding additional words can slow down the movement even more. A character "meandering aimlessly" across a room takes six syllables longer than one who "skips" or "darts" across the room.

Two-Minute Warm-Up

Write on the board: "How does a teapot speak as it comes to a boil?" It starts off coldly. Its feet begin to tickle. It warms up, feels funny, "burps" bubbles, becomes excited, and finally screams, "I'm ready!" Invite students to brainstorm other things that get faster or slower—popping popcorn on a stove; a rollercoaster ride; a wind-up toy winding down; an athlete tiring; a fire starting up, raging, dying out; a check-out line.

Activity

Ask students to write poems on subjects that change tempo. Guide them to arrange their words to help emphasize the message.

TEACHING TIP

To give your students another example of a poet's decision to choreograph words on the page, share this excerpt from the poem "Mystery" by Paul B. Janeczko.

One Friday night
Mom pulled out
Learning to Dance Is Fun
with diagrams of feet
and a long-play record,
while Dad watched,
like a patient
awaiting
the dentist's whining drill.

Mom counted softly
onetwo
onetwothree
through
    fox trot
       samba
          cha-cha-cha
as Dad danced—
feet on the wrong legs...

— Paul B. Janeczko

from the book *Brickyard Summer* (Orchard Books, 1989)

The Turtle

The turtle

takes . . one . . . . step

. . . and . . . . then

a-n-o-t-h-e-r.

. . . then he . . . slow-ly

. . looks . . . . around

. . . . . . and says,

"I don't . . . .

. . know . . . why . .

I . . . . . . b-o-t-h-e-r."

—Arnold Spilka

One Thing on My Mind

I've gottogotothebathroom

The bathroom the bathroom

I've gottogotothebathroom

Is all that I can say.

If Idon'tgettothererightaway

Right away right away

If Idon'tgettothererightaway

It will ruin the rest of my day.

—David Harrison

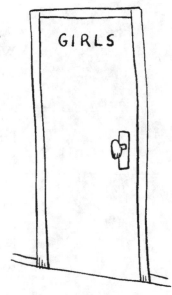

GIRLS

STRATEGY 14:
CHANGING TEMPO TO SUPPORT MEANING

Background

To help the reader sense a changing mood in a poem, poets sometimes choose words, or combinations of syllables, that subtly change the way the verse reads. That may involve changing the established rhythm a bit at just the right place the way Myra Cohn Livingston does in the poem on page 63. Her first stanza moves quickly, like a lighthearted song, but in the second she changes to a more thoughtful mood by selecting combinations of words that slow us down to think. "I look at it for a <u>long time</u>/And think of some/<u>Real good ways</u>." In Elizabeth Coatsworth's "The Sea Gull," the first two lines in each stanza only have six syllables while the third has eight, which makes us read faster to get them all into the pattern that has been established. The result sounds like a quick alarm, a warning to the unwary fish.

Two-Minute Warm-up

Why are vowels called "long" or "short"? Ask students to say the following words aloud: "bite" and "bit"; "goat" and "got"; "cute" and "cut." Can the students hear that the "long" vowels take slightly longer to say? If we string a few words together, the difference is more noticeable—"chickadee hops in little steps," with mostly short vowel sounds, moves across a line of poetry faster than "blue jay soars through the bleak night sky," even though both phrases are composed of eight syllables. Long vowels invite us to hold them as long as we want, but short vowels can sound odd when held out. (Lyricists know this. If you are holding a note forever at the end of the song, it's usually on a long vowel sound.) Poets can choose words with long or short vowel sounds as one subtle way to slow down or speed up the tempo of a poem.

Activity

Ask your students to look again at the poems they wrote for the previous lesson. Can they replace some of the words in these poems with words that further emphasize the changes in tempo portrayed in poems?

Martin Luther King

Got me a special place
For Martin Luther King.
His picture on the wall
Makes me sing.

I look at it for a long time
And think of some
Real good ways
We will overcome.

—Myra Cohn Livingston

Sea Gull

The sea gull curves his wings,
the sea gull turns his eyes.
Get down into the water, fish!
(if you are wise.)

The sea gull slants his wings,
the sea gull turns his head.
Get deep into the water, fish!
(or you'll be dead.)

—Elizabeth Coatsworth

STRATEGY 15:
MAKING UP WORDS

Background

Sometimes a real word just won't fit the bill. Lewis Carroll knew that when he wrote the Jabberwocky ("Twas brillig, and the slithy toves/Did gyre and gimble in the wabe"). Dr. Seuss specialized in Sneetches, Fiffer-feffer-feffs, Zax's, and such. And A. A. Milne's lovable bear was prone to make up words to go with his made-up songs. On page 65, Pooh Bear sings his new snow song to Piglet. When Piglet asks what "tiddely pom" means, Pooh says it's to make his song more hummy. And the *Man from Bottamus* on page 66 simply must have a lot of "mus's" to rhyme with hippopotamus. Made-up words can set the stage for silliness, supply a needed rhyme, or add a lively lilt to the cadence of the poem. Look for them in songs too.

Two-Minute Warm-up

Make up words with your kids. Hint: They needn't make sense. Examples: gadoop; ninino nana nonana; wala de wala; biddily.
Then link them to phrases, such as:

    There was on old dog/gadoop gadoop...

    Biddily biddily/apples and cream...

    Long ago and far away/Ninino nana nonana...

Activity

Write a group poem. As A.A. Milne did, choose as your subject an ordinary event, such as riding a bike or brushing teeth. Any action that has a repetition to it, and that kids know intimately, works especially well. Or, using "The Man From Bottamus" as a model, select an animal such as lioness or alligator and use it to build a nonsense rhyme scheme.
Note: Although the meanings of the words may be nonsense, their sounds can still be effective in a poem. Lewis Carrol's "Jabberwocky" may not make literal sense, but it certainly establishes a mood. After you've written your group poem, substitute different made-up words and talk about how the poem changes.

Outdoor Song Which Has to Be Sung in the Snow

The more it
SNOWS-tiddely-pom,
The more it
GOES-tiddely-pom
On
Snowing.

And nobody
KNOWS-tiddely-pom,
How cold my
TOES-tiddely-pom
How cold my
TOES-tiddely-pom
Are
Growing.

—A. A. Milne

The Man From Bottamus

There was a man from Bottamus

Who bought a hippopotamus.

Although it was a totamus,

It gobbled quite a lotamus.

The neighbors got upsotamus

And told him what they thoughtamus,

But he said, "I will notamus

Give up my hippopotamus!"

—David Harrison

Easy Poetry Lessons That Dazzle and Delight ● Scholastic Professional Books

STRATEGY 16:
RHYTHM

Background

The difference between meter and rhythm is the difference between how a line of poetry is written and how it is felt. Meter measures the beat of the syllables. Rhythm refers to how they flow. In "Love," on the next page, a combination of mostly anapests (da da DA) with iambs (da DA) gives the story of the green-eyed beetle the sort of rhythm I thought appropriate for such a romantic little fellow. John Frederick Nims writes: "In music, meter is what the metronome is doing: rhythm, what the composer or performer actually gives us. In poetry, meter...is the basic scheme, the da DA da DA.... Meter is like the abstract idea of a dance as a choreographer might plan it with no particular performers in mind; rhythm is like a dancer interpreting the dance in a personal way."

Two-Minute Warm-up

Read "Love" aloud twice. First, strictly the way the syllables are stressed, then the way you feel it should be read. The difference is rhythm. Ask your students to choose a favorite poem and try the same experiment. A good example to use would be Valerie Worth's "bell," on page 50.

Activity

Divide your class into pairs. Ask each team to select at least one poem that they think has a nice rhythm. Have one student read it aloud "straight" and the other read it the way the words seem to flow. Start a list of favorite selections.

Love

Said the green-eyed beetle

To his honey doodlebug,

"You're sweeter than a rose

And I want a little hug,"

So they hugged and they giggled

And a little later on

They had a thousand kids named

Green-Eyed Beetle

And Honey Doodlebug

And they all lived together

In a snug little rug.

—David Harrison

CHAPTER 4:
Patterns of Poetry

You don't have to know about poetry to enjoy poems. But unlike a magician, who hides the secrets to his success, the poet's tricks are all right there on the page in front of us. In this chapter we'll talk about a few of those tricks so that your students will recognize them in their favorite poems and learn to have fun with them.

In the study of life, there are two great kingdoms: animal and plant. In poetry, the two major divisions are verse and free verse. Verse is what we call metered language. It has structure, patterns, and regularities in form. (Free verse is not regular enough to be called verse but it is flexible enough to use various techniques or devices of verse.) With verse we pay attention to where the stressed syllables fall, how many there are in a line. We listen for sounds. We sense not only the meter but the rhythm of the words.

Verse generally conforms to specific formats known as forms or stanzas. From 2-line couplets to 14-line sonnets and even longer forms, there are rules to follow. As much fun as it is, even the lowly limerick requires that we observe certain basic rules. It has five lines; each frolics along more or less in a specific pattern of metrical units called "feet" with a set number of feet per line; and each line must end in a rhyme with specified other lines.

One way to learn to write limericks is by reading them, but most limericks that are written without understanding what makes them limericks aren't very good or much fun for young poets. Robert Frost said, "All the fun's in how you say a thing," and we want students to experience the fun of knowing how to write their own limericks.

Of the many standard forms of verse found among children's favorite poems, few rival the popularity of the 4-line stanza (or multiples of it). A short stanza is easy to remember, and the task of controlling the meter and arranging the rhymes is relatively simple. That's why this chapter also introduces 4-line and 8-line stanzas. First efforts at rhyming and following meter patterns may fall short of the mark but, like anything else, skill comes with practice.

Most poetry we remember from childhood rhymes. Some of our favorite nursery rhymes stem from a time when stories were told at camp meetings or in front of the fire before bedtime, a gentle reminder that poetry has been part of our lives since the beginning.

For this chapter we've selected poems that demonstrate the fun of poetry, both old and new. With guides like Ogden Nash, John Ciardi, Edward Lear, and Hilaire Belloc, you and your students are in for a jumping ride!

In this chapter we have introduced the six combinations of stressed and unstressed syllables that are most common in the English language. As you will discover on the following pages, we've scanned some of the poems to make it easier for you and your students to recognize the various combinations of the following:

⌣ = unstressed syllable

/ = stressed syllable

⌣ / (da Da) = iamb (Iambic foot)

⌣ ⌣ / (da da Da) = anapest (anapestic foot)

/ ⌣ (Da da) = trochee (trochaic foot)

/ ⌣ ⌣ (Da da da) = dactyl (dactylic foot)

/ / (Da Da) = spondee (spondaic foot)

⌣ ⌣ (da da) = pyrrhus (pyrrhic foot)

STRATEGY 17:
THE FOOT

Background

The English language has a certain beat.

Read that sentence again: (da DA da DA da DA da DA da DA).

Maybe 90 percent of poetry written in verse has that same beat. What's left falls mostly into three other patterns. Poets recognize these patterns and arrange their words into a "foot" according to the way we stress certain syllables when we pronounce them. The foot is a combination of syllables that forms the unit of measurement in a line of poetry. On the next page, you'll find examples of these four important patterns of poetry. [You can practice the patterns aloud with your kids.] The preceding sentence (in brackets), goes like this: da da DA da da DA da da DA da da DA, the same as in *A Visit from St. Nicholas*—or in a limerick.

Two-Minute Warm-up

On the board, make four columns: <u>da DA</u>, <u>da da DA</u>, <u>DA da</u>, and <u>DA da da.</u> Read aloud the poems on the next page, clearly emphasizing the accented syllables.

With your students, think of words (or combinations of syllables) that fall into each column.

da DA:	giraffe, the stars;
da da DA:	in the park; by the sea;
DA da:	lion, teacher;
DA da da:	wonderful, terrible.

Activity

Ask students to write one line for each of the four types of poetic feet. The lines can be of any length, and they don't have to go together. We're not looking for poems yet. We'll save that for the limerick in Strategy 19. For now, kids just need to "feel" the different beats.

(IAMBIC FEET—Accent Pattern: da DA da DA da DA)

The Farmer in the Dell

The farmer in the dell,

The farmer in the dell,

Hi ho the dairy-o,

The farmer in the dell.

(ANAPESTIC FEET—Accent Pattern: da da DA da da DA da da DA)

A Visit From St. Nicholas

Twas the night before Christmas, when all through the house

Not a creature was stirring, not even a mouse;

The stockings were hung by the chimney with care,

In hopes that St. Nicholas soon would be there;

—Clement Clarke Moore

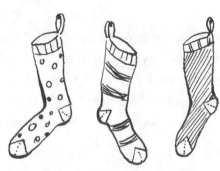

Easy Poetry Lessons That Dazzle and Delight ● Scholastic Professional Books

(TROCHAIC FEET—Accent Pattern: DA da DA da DA da)

Peter, Peter, Pumpkin Eater

Peter, Peter,

Pumpkin eater,

Had a wife

And couldn't keep her.

(DACTYLIC FEET—Accent Pattern: DA da da DA da da DA da da)

The Cat and the Fiddle

Hey diddle diddle,

The cat and the fiddle

NOTE: Sometimes a line breaks in the middle of a foot, as in *diddle* at the end of line one and *The* at the beginning of line two. In this case, the result is three dactylic feet followed by one trochaic foot.

STRATEGY 18:
THE COUPLET (EASY RHYME)

As your students progress in writing rhyming poetry, remind them not to "force" a rhyme (sticking a rhyming word at the end of a line even if it makes little sense in the poem). Sometimes, if no good word is available to complete a rhyme, the poet has to rearrange his first line so that it ends with a different word, a word easier to rhyme. For example, *I like my tea with lemon* might be a hard line to rhyme. *Lemon in my tea is what I like* would be easier, but *I like lemon in my tea* would offer even more rhyming possibilities.

TEACHING TIP

Background

Songs and poems that rhyme are among the first words that most children hear. "Pat a cake, pat a cake, baker's man, bake me a cake as fast as you can..." "Rain, rain, go away, come again some other day..." "Star light, star bright, first star I see tonight..." "Hickory dickory dock, the mouse ran up the clock...." Rhyming is a natural and basic element of our language, and a favorite with poets. The shortest form of traditional poetry is a couplet. A couplet has just two lines, which may rhyme or not. To write a limerick, we need to learn about couplets that rhyme. Reading those on page 75 will give your students the idea. **Hint:** Rhyming dictionaries help! But in a pinch poets make lists of words that rhyme with those we want to use.

Two-Minute Warm-up

List five one-syllable words across the board, for example: *day*, *see*, *eye*, *grow*, and *you*. See how many matching rhyme words your kids can think of quickly and add them to the lists.

Activity

Brainstorm together to make up at least one couplet from each of the five columns on the board. **Hint:** Don't worry about matching rhythm or length of lines. That comes in the next strategy. For now just focus on making up couplets and having fun with the rhymes.

The Crocus

da Da   da Da   da   Da   da Da
The golden crocus reaches up

da Da   da Da   da   Da   da Da
To catch a sunbeam in her cup.

—Walter Crane

When Little Frogs Hop

When little frogs hop

Their mothers yell, "Don't stop!"

—Arnold Spilka

The Crocus

The golden crocus reaches up

To catch a sunbeam in her cup.

—Walter Crane

Polar Bear

The secret of the polar bear

Is that he wears long underwear.

—Gail Kredenser

The Cow

The cow is of the bovine ilk;

One end is moo, the other, milk.

—Ogden Nash

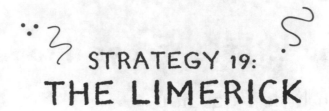

STRATEGY 19:
THE LIMERICK

Background

Now we're ready to write limericks. The general plan for the meter goes like this:

> da da DA da da DA da da DA
> da da DA da da DA da da DA
> da da DA da da DA
> da da DA da da DA
> da da DA da da DA da da DA

Each *da da DA* is a "foot." The number of feet per line looks like this: 3, 3, 2, 2, 3. Lines one and two form a couplet; lines three and four form a second couplet; and line five rhymes with the first two. **Important Hint:** Few limericks follow the meter perfectly. Below is an example:

THE GIANT   (rhyme scheme)

There once was a giant named Jones   a

Who lived in a castle of stones   a

And often, he said   b

"I'd sure like some bread   b

but I hate grinding up all these bones."   a

—David Harrison

But in spite of variations, what makes a limerick a limerick is that it "feels" like one: 1) The majority of its feet are anapests (da da DA); 2) Each line contains the usual number of accented feet (3, 3, 2, 2, 3); and 3) The rhyme scheme follows the plan (aabba).

Two-Minute Warm-up

Children find the classic opening "There once was..." easy to use, so have fun making up first lines, and list them on the board. **Hint:** Think about good rhyme words. For example: "There once was a teacher named Burke" could rhyme with work, smirk, lurk, irk, jerk, and quirk.

Activity

Divide the students into groups of five. Each student writes a first line of a limerick then, at your signal, passes it on to the next student in his group. Each student adds the second line to the poem he has been handed and then passes that poem on. The poems are always passed in the same direction. By the time five turns are completed, each group will have collaborated on five completed limericks. Each student can read aloud the poem that ends up in his hands. The sillier they are, the better. The originator of the limerick will be as surprised as anyone to hear how the poem evolved.

The Music Master

"My sons," said a Glurk slurping soup.

"We would make a fine musical group.

Put your spoon to your lip

And slurp when you sip.

But don't spill. Like this, children — *oop!*"

—John Ciardi

The Old Man With a Beard

There was an old man with a beard

Who said, "It is just as I feared! —

Two owls and a hen,

Four larks and a wren,

Have all built their nests in my beard!"

—Edward Lear

STRATEGY 20:
THE BALLAD STANZA

Background

Have you noticed how many poems are written in four lines? Four-line stanzas are called *quatrains* and they are the favorite English verse form. Though many variations are possible, the most common are the *ballad*, the *long ballad*, and the *short ballad*. All are generally written in iambic meter (da DA), although other kinds of feet may be substituted. The poems on the next page are examples of *ballads*. The pattern of feet per line alternates: 4, 3, 4, 3. In all ballads, the second and fourth lines end in a rhyme. In some, the first and third lines also end in a rhyme. Read the example ballads aloud to help establish the feel of the pattern of feet and rhyme.

Two-Minute Warm-Up

Help your class make up the first two lines of a ballad. Here's an example:

da DA da DA da DA da DA   A little mouse ran in the house,
da DA da DA da DA   The farmer grabbed a broom

Activity

Ask students to finish the ballad, either individually or in groups, as in:

> They ran upstairs and down again
> And through the living room.

Read the results aloud and talk about how many ways there can be to complete the same beginning. Change the farmer's broom to something else (pail, rake, sack) and see how that changes the ending.

A Wee Little Worm

A wee little worm in a hickory nut

Sang, happy as he could be,

"O I live in the heart of the whole round world,

And it all belongs to me!"

—James Whitcomb Riley

The Vulture

The Vulture eats between his meals

And that's the reason why

He very, very rarely feels

As well as you and I.

His eyes are dull, his head is bald,

His neck is growing thinner.

Oh! what a lesson for us all

To only eat at dinner!

—Hilaire Belloc

STRATEGY 21:
THE LONG BALLAD STANZA

Background

A long ballad is like a regular ballad except that every line has four feet (4, 4, 4, 4) instead of alternating 4, 3, 4, 3. Like the regular ballad, its rhymes may occur on the second and fourth lines (designated as abcb) and can also rhyme on the first and third as well (abab). But this form can be (and frequently is) written in couplets (aabb), which adds flexibility. The long ballad by Charlotte Zolotow, on page 82, is an example of all four lines having the same rhyme (aaaa). The other examples are written in couplets. As you can see, even though the long ballad shares much in common with the regular ballad, their subtle differences set them apart.

Two-Minute Warm-up

Set up the first two lines of meter for a long ballad on a piece of chart paper and work together to make up a good beginning. Couplets may offer the best way to get started.

da DA da DA da DA da DA	My mother cooked a brussels sprout,
da DA da DA da DA da DA	My little brother threw it out,

Activity

Finish the class-written ballad and display it so students can use it for reference. Have students choose a rhyme pattern and write a ballad of their own.

River Winding

Rain falling, what things do you grow?

Snow melting, where do you go?

Wind blowing, what trees do you know?

River winding, where do you flow?

—Charlotte Zolotow

River Winding

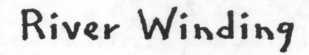

Rain falling, what things do you grow?

Snow melting, where do you go?

Wind blowing, what trees do you know?

River winding, where do you flow?

—Charlotte Zolotow

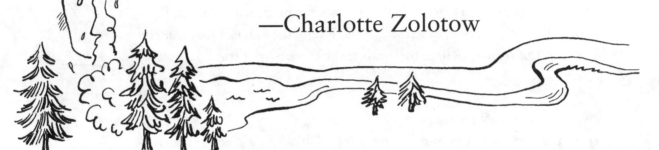

The Little Man

As I was walking up the stair

I met a man who wasn't there;

He wasn't there again today.

I wish, I wish he'd stay away.

—Hughes Mearns

The Lizard

The Lizard is a timid thing

That cannot dance or fly or sing;

He hunts for bugs beneath the floor

And longs to be a dinosaur.

—John Gardner

A Sad Tale

Here lie the bones of Byron Biggers,

Eaten alive by hungry chiggers,

So if you see poor Byron twitch,

Scratch his bones 'cause they still itch.

—David Harrison

STRATEGY 22:
THE SHORT BALLAD STANZA

Background

A short ballad is like a regular ballad except that the number of feet per line is 3, 3, 4, 3 instead of 4, 3, 4, 3. A line of three beats is called *trimeter* ('trim-e-ter); four beats makes it *tetrameter* (te-'tram-e-ter). The short ballad's rhyme scheme is usually <u>abcb</u>, meaning that only the second and fourth lines end in a rhyme. The examples on page 84 include short ballads of one and two stanzas. Now that we've introduced all three ballad forms, your students can search for them in their favorite books and share their prizes in class. Consider a Ballad of the Week contest with students voting on their favorite Regular, Long, and Short Ballad poems.

Two-Minute Warm-up

Write four lines of short ballad meter on the board, then work together to make up a good beginning, using the example provided or one of your own.

da DA da DA da DA   My sister ate the dog,
da DA da DA da DA   My sister ate the cat,
da DA da DA da DA da DA
da DA da DA da DA

Activity

Ask kids to complete the short ballad begun by the group. Read the results aloud and encourage suggestions for improvement.

Beside the Line of Elephants

I think they had no pattern

When they cut out the elephant's skin;

Some places it needs letting out,

And others, taking in.

—Edna Becker

Who Has Seen the Wind?

Who has seen the wind?

Neither I nor you:

But when the leaves hang trembling,

The wind is passing through.

Who has seen the wind?

Neither you nor I:

But when the leaves bow down their heads,

The wind is passing by.

—Christina Rossetti

STRATEGY 23:
THE 8-LINE STANZA

Background

There are several varieties of 8-line stanzas, known collectively as *octaves* ('ak-tivs), but the most popular amounts to two 4-line stanzas joined together. This form typically follows a pattern of lines with the same number of feet, although that number may vary. The typical rhyme scheme is <u>abcbdefe</u> (2nd & 4th lines rhyme; 6th & 8th lines rhyme) or <u>ababcdcd</u> (rhymes occur in lines 1 & 3, 2 & 4, 5 & 7, and 6 & 8). A rule of thumb difference between an 8-line stanza and two 4-liners is that some poems simply read better if they are told in eight continuous lines.

Two-Minute Warm-up

Modeling is helpful in learning longer forms. Choose an 8-line poem such as "A Stripeless Tiger." Write the first four lines on the board, and brainstorm other ways to describe why the "tiger" is really an elephant: can't climb a tree, sleep on a limb, etc.

Activity

Provide time in class and at home to work out individual endings (last four lines) of the poem. If your kids are enjoying the longer form, see what they can do with their own ideas. Read them aloud and discuss suggestions for improvement. Some kids might be more comfortable finding octaves in books to share.

A Stripeless Tiger

A stripeless tiger

That's an elephant's size,

With an elephant's trunk

And an elephant's eyes,

That tries to roar

But somehow can't—

Most probably is

Just an elephant.

—Arnold Spilka

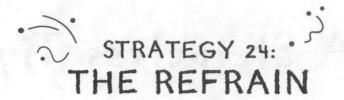

STRATEGY 24:
THE REFRAIN

Background

Many poems depend on repetition of certain phrases, lines, or groups of lines to make a point. When they fall at the same place—normally at the end but sometimes at the beginning—they're called *refrains*. Valine Hobbs, in the poem "One Day When We Went Walking" on page 89 begins each stanza with a strong refrain that lets us know something exciting is about to happen. It's like hearing a story begin, "Once upon a time…." Notice how the poet changes the final refrain to set us up for the punch line. Judith Viorst's poem, "Since Hanna Moved Away," page 102, depends on a refrain at the end of each stanza to emphasize the sadness of losing a friend, whereas I turned to an end refrain in "This One Night of the Year" for comic effect.

Two-Minute Warm-up

Make a quick list on the board of catchy phrases or lines that would make interesting refrains: *one day when I went flying; and that was the end of that; and we never saw Sally again; seems to me.*

Activity

Ask each student to choose a refrain line from the board and use it as the beginning or ending of the stanzas in a poem. Compare the poems written around each refrain to show how many ways poets can use the same idea. You could even select a single refrain for the whole class. Each poem will still turn out differently.

One Day When We Went Walking

One day when we went walking,
   I found a dragon's tooth,
   A dreadful dragon's tooth.
   "A locust thorn," said Ruth.

One day when we went walking,
   I found a brownie's shoe,
   A brownie's button shoe.
   "A dry pea pod," said Sue.

One day when we went walking,
   I found a mermaid's fan,
   A merry mermaid's fan.
   "A scallop shell," said Dan.

One day when we went walking,
   I found a fairy's dress,
   A fairy's flannel dress.
   "A mullein leaf," said Bess.

Next time that I go walking —
   Unless I meet an elf,
   A funny, friendly elf —
   I'm going by myself!

   —Valine Hobbs

This One Night of the Year

I try to overcome my fear
(At least this one night of the year)
When glowing skeletons appear...

"Trick or treat!"

Monsters stagger down the street,
Mummies wrap in a tattered sheet,
And fairies dance on tennis-shoed feet...

"Trick or treat!"

Goblins lurch and leopards scratch,
Pumpkins leave their pumpkin patch,
And eager hands reach out to snatch...

"Trick or treat!"

Muffled voices! Rustling wings!
They've sniffed me out! My doorbell rings!
"Boo! Shoo, you scary things!"

"Trick or treat!"

—David Harrison

CHAPTER 5:
Finding Ideas

K ids always want to know, "Where do you find ideas?"—as if they were Easter eggs or Leprechaun gold. That really isn't the right question. Even if you have a good idea, what are you going to do with it? A better question would be, "How do you get started?" The answer to that one is easy. There are so many ways to get started, we could have filled this book with them. Instead we selected proven techniques to present in this chapter.

Often a poem can begin with some catchy phrase that passes uninvited through the poet's thought. For me it's sometimes a rhythm. Perhaps I'll see a headline in the newspaper which, when read aloud, takes on an interesting cadence that makes me want to try writing something like that. Most of us who write all the time don't rely on anything in particular to get us started. As often as not, we're aware of how it happens only after the fact, if we pause to examine what occurred.

That's how most of the strategies in this chapter developed: after they had worked for someone. Individually, your students will probably like some better than others. They're not presented in any sort of sequence. You can take them up in whatever order you prefer and skip any that don't seem right for your group. We offer them simply as classroom-tested methods of getting thoughts onto paper.

STRATEGY 25:
MAKING ASSOCIATIONS

Background

"What are you thinking about?" asks a friend. "A million things," we respond when our thoughts seem to be hopping about like rabbits. But those rabbits may be related. When someone says something—it could be as simple as "take a right at the next corner,"—or when we see something—something as ordinary as a gum wrapper on the ground—it may trigger dozens of associations that can be the ingredients of a poem. For example, once in a grocery store I passed a display of potatoes. They made me think of salt, butter, bacon bits, and sour cream. People stopped to buy potatoes. Some were overweight and could use a little diet. So could I. By the time I got home, "The Perfect Diet" was already taking shape in my mind. The connection hopped in a straight line: potatoes—fattening food—overweight people—diet. Poems often begin that way, by allowing our mind to wonder as it wanders.

Two-Minute Warm-up

• Put a word on the board, such as *turtle*.
• Invite children to tell you all the words that spring to mind and list these on the board.
• Now ask children to choose one of the words they've brainstormed and write a second column of ideas related to that.
• Now have kids choose an association from the second column and brainstorm ideas related to it.

Activity

Ask children to let their minds bounce from one thing to another. When they come to an idea they like, they can write a poem about it. Encourage them to use the listing technique outlined in the warm-up to help them brainstorm. Once they've arrived at their topic, they might want to look back at how they got there and use some of the transitional links for images in the poem.

TURTLE
poky, shell, shy, ancient, patient, reptile.

POKY
getting out of bed, week before Christmas, last month of school

GETTING OUT OF BED
missing the bus, brother pulling my toe, losing my shoe.

92

The Perfect Diet

Mrs. LaPlump weighed 300 pounds
And her husband weighed 202.
"I've got to lose some weight," she said,
"I'll give up potatoes and pizza and bread,"
And Mr. LaPlump said, "I will, too,
My darling, I'll do it for you."

So each of them lost 100 pounds
And he only weighed 102.
"I've got to lose more weight," she said.
"This next 100," said he, "I dread,
For when we are finished I'll only weigh 2,
But darling, I'll do it for you."

So they lost another 100 pounds
And her figure was perfect and trim,
But there is a lesson here I think
'Cause Mr. LaPlump continued to shrink
Till one day he disappeared down the sink,
And you may find that grim, my dears,
But that was the end of him.

—David Harrison

STRATEGY 26:
FIGURES OF SPEECH

Background

English is full of idioms and clichés which we use to enliven our conversation. *I could eat a horse. He's grown a foot. She was green with envy. His bark is worse than his bite.* Such expressions offer excellent hunting grounds for humorous poems. Think about what could happen if they were literally true! Then write about the results. *I'm so hungry I could eat a horse* made me imagine a couple of little girls with enormous appetites, looking for a juicy horse to gobble. "I'd hate to be the horse," I decided. The result was "My Advice," on the next page. Thinking about *you've grown a foot*, I asked myself, What if someone grew a real foot instead of twelve inches? "How Willy Grew" was my answer.

Two-Minute Warm-up

See how many expressions your class can think of in a short time.

Activity

Invite your kids to have fun writing poems that take an expression literally. Illustrate them and display them around the room, or collect them in a book. Read some aloud. For inspiration, share with children the book of idioms *The King Who Rained* by Fred Gwynne (Simon & Schuster, 1988).

Easy Poetry Lessons That Dazzle and Delight ● Scholastic Professional Books

My Advice

Elizabeth Ann and Betty Lou Morse
Said, "We're so hungry
We could eat a horse!"
So my advice, if you're a horse, is
Whatever you do,
Avoid the Morses.

—David Harrison

How Willy Grew

Willy was smaller than the other boys,
But his mother said, "Son, don't fret,
One of these days you'll grow a foot,
You'll catch those big boys yet."
And sure enough, Willy grew a foot,
But not like his mother said.
Whatever it was had five little toes,
And it stuck right out of his head.

—David Harrison

STRATEGY 27:
SLEUTHING FOR IDEAS

Background

I saw the famous ballet star Edward Vilella captivate an audience of boys, many of whom figured it was "sissy stuff" to dance on one's toes. He sold them on the energy such dancing requires, the physical condition, the athletic ability, the strength. They hadn't thought about all the action involved. I like to surprise students with aspects of writing poetry they haven't thought about, such as sleuthing for ideas. Like detectives searching for clues, students observe details that "mere mortals" pass by. Journals become important, as poetry sleuths jot down quick thoughts and "brilliant flashes of insight" during a busy day. Who knows where the next poetry ideas will turn up? Never let it be said that writing poetry isn't exciting! Joyce Pyle's fifth graders went sleuthing at a nursing home then wrote poems about what they discovered there. Their examples are on page 97.

Two Minute Warm-up

Brainstorm ideas that poetry sleuths might want to investigate. Take, for example, kids climbing off the bus in the morning and back on in the afternoon. Do they act different? Look different? Sound different? Do they hurry more to get off or to get back on? Everday activities may hold amazing facts for enterprising poetry sleuths.

Activity

Form teams of poetry detectives (with appropriate names) and "send them on assignment" for a week. During that time their information must be kept top secret. Spies can be everywhere. But on the big day, their reports ought to be filled with intriguing facts and the seeds of poems.

Bob and Me

I'd sit on his knee.
All of a sudden his knee is a horse
And I'm galloping away in a
　　　horse race.

When the race is over
he'd tuck me under my sheets and
　　give me a kiss.
　　(After all, he's my grandpa)

　　　　　—Jennie McGraw

Grandma's House

The little mint-green house
　　Set back off the road
Expecting me every second.

Lonely and wanting attention
The house isn't much
But, what's inside is worth a lot
　　To me.

—Anna Steury

Hey, It's Reba!

What's that?
Hey, it's Reba!
Dancing her fingers
across the piano keys.

One note
of that old Alley Cat
and she lifts our souls.

People start swaying
and humming the tune.
What's that?
Hey, it's Reba!

—Jennifer Wilkinson

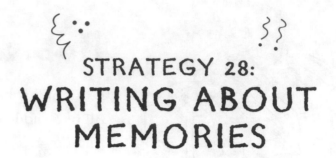

STRATEGY 28:
WRITING ABOUT MEMORIES

Background

Favorite moments and special events stick to our memories. Some grow into stories that we share when we have an appreciative audience. I tell students of the night I ate too many tacos and was sent home from school the next day still reeking of garlic; of moving away and leaving my cat behind; of fooling my mother with a toy snake. Students sympathize. They understand. They also have eaten too much, lost a pet, fooled their mother. I tell them how to write about what they remember in three steps: Think about it, talk about it, write about it. Talking (describing the memory to someone) helps us remember details and put the event into a logical sequence. Writing about it then becomes much easier, almost like reporting.

Two-Minute Warm-up

Ask kids to recall their very first memory—the earliest image in their life they can remember. In searching back in time, they'll probably journey through many memories. Have them write down key words to remind them of any of the memories along the way that strike them as especially important or pleasing.

Activity

Once they find that first memory, ask them to use it—or one of the others they've noted on their list, if they have a strong preference—to try to pull up as many detailed images as they can to write a poem.

ANOTHER

long
drawn-out
night
another
bitter, brutal
fight.
Time
stood still
till
morning
broke
with a
trembling
throbbing
terrored-force
as
I woke up
sleepily
half-believing
I hadn't
heard
the
dreaded
word—
divorce.

—Lee Bennett Hopkins

LEAVING CORKY

I stand with the car door open.
"Corky!" I call out across the fields.
"Here kitty kitty kitty kitty!"

"Time to go."
Dad's voice is quiet.
"Just one more hour," I beg.
"He's been gone a month already," he says.
"Probably chewed up again."

The car eases down the dirt drive.
I stare out the window,
leaving a mind trail,
but in my heart I know.

I'll never see him again,
never know if he's alive,
never be able to explain.

Leaving Corky,
I'm too sad to cry.

—David Harrison

Easy Poetry Lessons That Dazzle and Delight ● Scholastic Professional Books

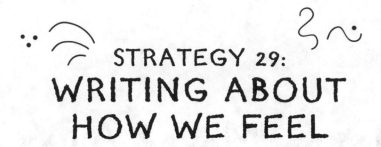

STRATEGY 29:
WRITING ABOUT HOW WE FEEL

Background

Human emotions are universal. We all, at some time, feel happy…
sad…worried…relieved…frightened…angry. Relating emotions to experi-
ences (real or imagined) provides us with a rich source for writing. Two
powerful examples are presented on the next two pages: Judith Viorst
reminds us of the pain of having a best friend move away; Dorothy Aldis
deals with the awfulness of being lost.

Two-Minute Warm-up

Ask your students how the character in "Since Hanna Moved Away"
feels. Now have them look through the poem to find words that directly
describe those feelings—words like "sad" or "lonely". There are none.
(Even "grouchy" refers to the color of the sky, not to the speaker.) Then
how *does* the poet express her character's feelings? She writes unique sensory images to *reflect* those feelings. For example, she describes the character's attitudes and actions ("I won't come out").

Activity

Have students write a poem about an emotional event in their lives. It can
be happy, sad, whatever they choose. Remind them of the power of
images to portray emotions in a fresh, effective way.

Since Hanna Moved Away

The tires on my bike are flat.
The sky is grouchy gray.
At least it sure feels like that
Since Hanna moved away.

Chocolate ice cream tastes like prunes.
December's come to stay.
They've taken back the Mays and Junes
Since Hanna moved away.

Flowers smell like halibut.
Velvet feels like hay.
Every handsome dog's a mutt
Since Hanna moved away.

Nothing's fun to laugh about.
Nothing's fun to play.
They call me, but I won't come out
Since Hanna moved away.

—Judith Viorst

When I Was Lost

Underneath my belt

My stomach was a stone.

Sinking was the way I felt.

And hollow.

And Alone.

—Dorothy Aldis

STRATEGY 30:
WRITING ABOUT NATURE

Background

One of our greatest sources of inspiration is nature. A trellis of red roses pulls us to a stop in our busy day, at least long enough to marvel at the beauties of the world we live in. We look with amusement at a tiny bug dragging home a meal ten times its size. We shudder at the might of nature's temper tantrums. When Lillian Morrison stands at the edge of the roaring sea and thinks of water tigers taking great bites of the shore, she is using a metaphor of nature to describe nature. Read this poem and favorites of your own to demonstrate how poets turn to nature again and again for the subjects of their works.

Two-Minute Warm-up

Take a nature hike if possible. If not, ask students to bring in a natural object or a picture from nature. Display them in the room. Supply some of your own. Let students choose an object to write about.

Activity

Natural things live interesting lives. Plants and animals have actual life cycles, but even rocks have stories to tell. Have your students write a poem from the point of view of something in nature. Imagine what it's like to be a tree or a cloud, a snail or a field of corn.

TEACHING TIP

Ask students if they notice anything about the shape of the poem "Breakers." Because of the lengths of the lines, the poem actually looks like waves, washing onto the shore, retracting, then washing onto the shore again.

Breakers

Roaring,

all flowing grace,

the water tigers pounce,

feed on the shore,

worry it

again and again,

take great bites

they cannot swallow

and leave the toothmarks

of their long white fangs.

—Lillian Morrison

CHAPTER 6:
Revising Poems

I f there's a secret to good writing, it's this: The harder we work, the easier it looks. If we read something and tell ourselves, "I could have written that," the writer has probably spent long hours of effort to make us feel that way.

Writers learn, eventually, that our first draft is not likely to be our best. Revision is a natural part of composing our thoughts, determining what we want to say and how we'll say it. The first draft of this chapter began:

> *Doctors practice medicine. Lawyers practice law. Writers practice writing. The more we practice the better we become, and that's especially easy to see in our writing, as draft after draft improves our final product.*

That sounded stuffy and didactic. I began again, this way:

> *If we read something and tell ourselves, "I could have written that," the writer has probably spent long hours of effort to make us feel that way. If there's a secret to good writing, it's this: The harder we work, the easier it looks.*

The second sentence was stronger than the first, so I switched their order. This sort of trial and error composition is so basic that we may not even recognize it as rewriting, but it is, and it's vitally important. Whether we are writing a term paper, a short story, or a poem, we must establish a point of view that will carry our message in a clear and consistent manner. False starts like those above help us decide what we want to say and what we do *not* want to say. Novelists sometimes write a chapter or two before discovering the point where their story truly begins, then discard everything prior to that point. We did something similar with this book, which took more than two years to develop. We organized our thoughts and wrote them in various ways before settling on this format.

Such general revising is only the beginning, of course. So that our readers can see clearly what we have to say, we must polish every thought until it sparkles. When writers revise, we probably don't do it in an organized, step-one, step-two way. We just read and react: This stays, that goes. But to assist young writers, we have devised a checklist that takes some of the mystery out of the process.

We even have an acronym for it: SCRIPT (Sequence, Content, Rhythm, Interest, Pet words, and Title). Hopefully, your kids will want to turn their writing into SCRIPT when they're done.

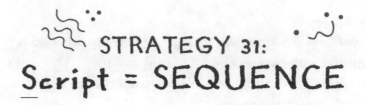

STRATEGY 31:
Script = SEQUENCE

Background

Sometimes I'm horrified by my first draft, when the words have tumbled out the way they might in conversation: breathlessly and formlessly. Thank goodness for the chance to revise! The *logical* sequence of what we say is so important that we place it first in the process of rewriting. Whether young poets are composing in verse or in free verse, they need to make sure that their work makes sense to the reader. Knowing that adult writers struggle with the same problem, and solve it in the same way, helps students understand that nothing—neither rhyme, nor meter, nor the way the line breaks—can save a thought that is poorly said.

Two-Minute Warm-up

Take a favorite poem and turn it into prose. See what the sequence is.

Activity

Go back to the very first poem the class wrote together—discussed in the Group Poem strategy on page 32. Discuss the sequence you chose then. Rearrange the lines so that the poem progresses in a different way— starts quietly and gets louder; starts fast and gets slower; starts with few references to people, ends with a crowd. If you grouped similar images in one stanza, split them up and spread them throughout the poem. Talk about how each different arrangement yields a different poem. What do you want this poem to say? What story do you want it to tell? Through what experience do you want to lead the reader? Through which arrangement does the poem best achieve your goal?

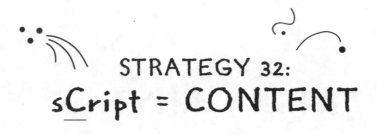

STRATEGY 32:
sCript = CONTENT

Background

In a novel, we might have 50,000 words to tell our story; in a short story, maybe 1,500; s a poem, perhaps 50. Yet for all three we must answer the same question: What do we want to tell our reader? Group poems and list poems are good practice for budding poets, because we begin by making lists of everything we can think of about the subject. Putting the poem together, then, requires that we decide what should go into the finished product and what should be left out. Reread the collaborative poem "On the Playground" in Strategy 2. Before they wrote, the kids must have had fun thinking about the sights, sounds, and smells of their own playground.

Two-Minute Warm-up

Come up with a topic (the circus, a family, the space shuttle) and have students suggest anything and everything the topic brings to mind. Again, the idea is to open the mind and let spill out a flood of any images and associations that might provide material for a poem.

Activity

Look again at the group poem you wrote. If you came up with a different sequence in the last strategy, the new arrangement may call for different or additional material. Perhaps some of the original lines are no longer appropriate. In a poem every word should make a contribution—don't get so attached to a good line that you leave it in if it doesn't serve the poem. You can always save it and use it in another poem. In fact, review the material the class rejected when you first created the group poem; some of it may be just right now.

STRATEGY 33:
scRipt = RHYTHM

Background

As we discussed in Strategy 17, the English language has a beat to it. In
verse poetry it's mostly iambic (da DA da DA da DA), but there are other
patterns as well. Poets combine those patterns of speech into various
combinations. But when we read a poem aloud, we also feel something
else: its rhythm, the way the words flow together. Rhythm can be personal, in the same sense that no two singers interpret a song quite alike. A
native of Alabama reading a poem written by a New Englander may
interpret the rhythm of the lines somewhat differently from the way of
the poet. But a poem (unless it's written in free verse) should also convey
some universal sense of rhythm that we all can enjoy, no matter where we
live. Therefore, an important step in rewriting is to work out the natural
flow of our words.

Two-Minute Warm-up

Read some poems aloud, asking the class to pay particular attention to the
flow of the poems—where they pause, where they move smoothly, speed
up, slow down.

Activity

Read your Group Poem aloud. Is it easy to read the poem aloud or do
some of the lines trip up the reader? Is it fun to listen to? Does the flow of
the words reinforce what the words are saying? If the action in a stanza is
fast, do the lines also skip along briskly? If a slower tempo seems more
appropriate to the meaning, can you use punctuation, line breaks, different
word choices, different arrangements of words, to slow down the passage?

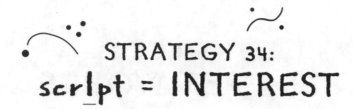

STRATEGY 34:
script = INTEREST

Background

Revising to improve the interest level of our writing can be difficult because writers tend to fall in love with everything we write. Of course it's interesting! I wrote it! Sadly, our readers may not always agree, and a bored reader usually quits reading. Some key questions to ask ourselves about our writing are: Is my work fun to read? Is it lively? Does it need dialogue? Would a metaphor/simile help? Do I need fresher words? Is it interesting? Writers learn to ask ourselves these questions and try to answer them as honestly as possible. If we don't, our readers may answer them for us.

Two-Minute Warm-up

Invite students to describe what makes a poem interesting. Use their language to make a checklist to post on the wall and for them to keep in their notebooks. The list may include technical terms like *rhymes, metaphor, onomatopoeia, assonance* and more general considerations like *honesty, surprise, clarity,* and *humor.*

Activity

Apply the checklist to your Group Poem to see if further revisions can be made. Then have your students look again at poems they've written. What might they do to make their work more interesting? Ask students to share their changes with the class.

STRATEGY 35:
scriPt = PET WORDS and CLICHÉS

Background

Most of us develop three vocabularies: one for conversation, one for writing, and one for reading. Speaking, we think more of what to say than how. Writing provides time to improve the how. Reading, we discover new words which, like exotic blossoms, add unexpected color to our thoughts. The first draft of a manuscript tends to read the way we speak: a weedy garden entangled by clichés, pet adjectives, and lazy verbs. Leaping at once into such a thicket, shoving our way from first draft to last, is scratchy work; safer to slow down, snip our way through. By seizing a sharp pencil and pruning away lackluster language, we give good ideas a better chance to flourish.

Two-Minute Warm-up

Put up some typical "speaking" vocabulary words and expressions, and ask for more colorful choices. Like this:

As <u>sweet</u> [as <u>sugar</u>]	...as a mouthful of honey
	...as hot buttered corn
<u>Silly</u>	nutty, wacky, goofy, daffy, loony, batty
As <u>frisky</u> [as a <u>puppy</u>]	...as ponies in May
	...as a wagon of kittens
<u>Run</u>	sprint, dash, rush, plunge, scurry

Activity

Look again at your Group Poem for any pet words or expressions that might be replaced with fresher language. Have students examine some of their own poems. For students who want help in finding more creative ways to express an image, list the phrases on the board and have the class brainstorm for better choices.

STRATEGY 36:
scripT = TITLE

Background

Sometimes titles come first. Once I dreamed of a good title—*Detective Bob and the Great Ape Escape*—and then wrote a book to go with it. But often the best title may not become clear until the poem is nearly done. The title tells how we feel about the poem and what we want the reader to expect. It helps set the mood, create interest, and sometimes becomes part of the first line. Since we make so many changes during the writing process, it usually pays to wait until the poem is complete to make a final choice.

Two-Minute Warm-up

Hand out copies of "My Cat" on page 114 and ask students why Barbara Esbensen may have chosen the title she did. Her cat in the poem *seems* harmless and still while he naps (though we see by the end that he's a coiled spring). Like the cat, the title is quiet and undramatic, which has helped to lull the reader, like an unsuspecting mouse, so the ending is more of a surprise.

Activity

Read some titles from a poetry anthology to your class. Which title intrigues the students, makes them want to read the poem? What expectations does the title create in their minds? Now read the poem aloud, and discuss if it met the expectations raised by the title. If not, was the title misleading? Do you think the poet did that on purpose? What other titles could this poem have, and how would they contribute to the poem? Ask students to re-examine poems they have written. Could a different title make the poem even more effective? How about the Group Poem you've been revising? If it has changed substantially, perhaps it needs a new title.

My Cat

My cat is asleep—white paws
folded under
his chin He is a soft gray
smudge on the round rug

Dozing in the sun
He is a warm round stone
with a fur collar

My cat is taking
a nap Not a whisker
trembles Not a hair
moves His breath goes
softly in and out

Stay in your holes
mice! My cat sees you
in his dream
and he has left
his motor running!

—Barbara Juster Esbensen

Easy Poetry Lessons That Dazzle and Delight ● Scholastic Professional Books

References

Behn, Robin and Chase Twichell. *The Practice of Poetry*. New York: Harper Perennial, 1992.

Beum, Robert and Karl Shapiro. *A Prosody Handbook*. New York: HarperCollins, 1965.

Bishop, Wendy. *Working Words: the Process of Creative Writing*. Mayfield Publishing Company, 1992.

Cook, Roy J. *One Hundred and One Famous Poems. An Anthology*. Chicago: The Cable Company, 1929.

Cullinan, Bernice E., Marilyn C. Scala, and Virginia C. Schroder. *Three Voices: An Invitation to Poetry Across the Curriculum*. York, Maine: Stenhouse, 1995.

Deutsch, Babette. *Poetry Handbook: A Dictionary of Terms*. Fourth Edition. New York: Funk & Wagnalls, 1974.

Fletcher, Ralph. *What a Writer Needs*. Portsmouth, New Hampshire: Heinemann, 1993.

— *Live Writing: Breathing Life Into Your Words*. New York: Avon/Camelot, 1999.

Fussell, Paul. *Poetic Meter & Form*. Revised Edition. New York: McGraw-Hill, 1979.

Hulme, Joy N. and Donna Guthrie. *How to Write, Recite, and Delight in All Kinds of Poetry*. Millbrook, 1996.

Janeczko, Paul B. *How to Write Poetry*. New York: Scholastic, 1999.

Jerome, Judson. *Poet's Handbook*. Cincinnati, Ohio: Writer's Digest Books, 1980.

Nims, John Frederick. *Western Wind: An Introduction to Poetry*. Second Edition. New York: Random House, 1983.

Schaken, Peter and Jack Ridl. *Approaching Poetry: Perspectives and Responses*. New York: St. Martin's Press, 1997.

Wallace, Robert and Michelle Boisseau. *Writing Poems*. Fourth Edition. New York: HarperCollins College Publishers, 1996.

Williams, Miller. *Patterns of Poetry: An Encyclopedia of Forms*. Baton Rouge, LA and London: Louisiana State University Press, 1986.

Glossary
Terms and Correlations

An old song tells us, the toe bone is connected to the foot bone and the foot bone is connected to the ankle bone. In poetry, we might sing "the syllable is connected to the foot and the foot is connected to the line." This flow chart attempts to connect some of the common elements of verse (structured poetry) to help you navigate your own study of poetry and plan lessons for your students. The books listed on page 115 are good resources to guide you too. Though some of the concepts of structured poetry may be too difficult for elementary students to master, your knowing them will nonetheless enrich your approach to teaching poetry.

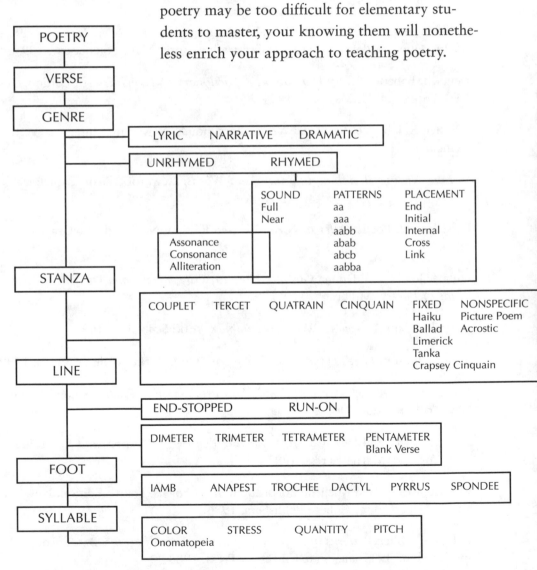

POETRY

VERSE

GENRE

LYRIC   NARRATIVE   DRAMATIC

UNRHYMED   RHYMED

SOUND	PATTERNS	PLACEMENT
Full	aa	End
Near	aaa	Initial
	aabb	Internal
	abab	Cross
	abcb	Link
	aabba	

Assonance
Consonance
Alliteration

STANZA

COUPLET	TERCET	QUATRAIN	CINQUAIN	FIXED	NONSPECIFIC
				Haiku	Picture Poem
				Ballad	Acrostic
				Limerick	
				Tanka	
				Crapsey Cinquain	

LINE

END-STOPPED   RUN-ON

DIMETER	TRIMETER	TETRAMETER	PENTAMETER
			Blank Verse

FOOT

IAMB   ANAPEST   TROCHEE   DACTYL   PYRRUS   SPONDEE

SYLLABLE

COLOR	STRESS	QUANTITY	PITCH
Onomatopeia			

The Study of Poetry

The study of poetry can be divided into Prosody and Semantics. Prosody includes anything that can be measured: meter, line, stanza. Semantics grapples with the unmeasurable: ideas, words, logic. We include this table to assist you in leading discussions about poetry and helping students tackle the process of revising.

SEMANTICS	PROSODY
Idea	Meter
Words	Line
Logic	Stanza
Connection	Tempo
Connotation	Rhythm
Imagery	Sound
Metaphor	Pause
Simile	Rhyme
	Rhymelessness
	Color
	Pitch
	Stress

ACROSTIC

A poem in which the first letter of each line, read down the page, spells out a message or name. The final letters may also spell out a message. More complex patterns may involve a succession: first letter of the first line, second letter of the second, etc.

ALLITERATION

The relationship between words when consonants just before the first accented vowels are the same, the vowels are not pronounced alike, and the following consonants are different. Examples: sweep/swallow; lick/line; leap/lad; follow/furry/feet.

ANAPESTIC

A combination of two unstressed syllables followed by one stressed syllable (da da DA da da DA da da DA). A pattern made up primarily of these anapests is anapestic. Examples: in the night; through the house; little girl.

ASSONANCE

The relationship between words when same or similar vowel sounds are sandwiched between different consonants. Example: hit/will; disturb/bird; cat/sad.

BALLAD, LONG

A four line stanza where all four lines are iambic tetrameter (four sets of da DA), and the rhyme scheme is generally *abab* (first and third lines end in a rhyme; second and fourth lines end in a rhyme), *abcb* (only the second and fourth lines end in a rhyme), or *aabb* (first and second lines end in a rhyme; third and fourth lines end in a rhyme).

BALLAD, REGULAR

A four line stanza where lines one and three are iambic tetrameter (four sets of da DA) and lines two and four are iambic trimeter (three sets of da DA), and the rhyme scheme is generally *abab* (first and third lines end in a rhyme; second and fourth lines end in a rhyme) or *abcb* (only the second and fourth lines end in a rhyme).

BALLAD, SHORT

A four line stanza where lines one, two, and four are iambic trimeter (three sets of da DA) and line three is tetrameter (four sets of da DA), and the rhyme scheme is usually *abcb* (only the second and fourth lines end in a rhyme).

BLANK VERSE

Unrhymed, usually written in iambic pentameter (five sets of da DA). The most widely used verse form of English poetry; the language of Shakespeare, Milton, and Wordsworth.

CINQUAIN

A stanza of five lines. Pronounced /sin-kane; far less common than four line stanzas (quatrains). Examples include limerick, tanka, and the Crapsey model, all described alphabetically.

CONSONANCE

The relationship between words when consonants just before and following vowels that are not pronounced alike are the same. Example: truck/trick; trance/trounce.

COUPLET

A stanza of two lines, the simplest of English stanzas. It may rhyme or not and has been in continuous use since the fifteenth century.

CRAPSEY CINQUAIN

A five line stanza form developed by Adelaide Crapsey and published, after her death, in 1915. It normally consists of 2, 4, 6, 8, and 2 syllables, respectively, which are usually unrhymed.

CROSS RHYME

Rhyme that occurs when the syllable at the end of a line rhymes with a syllable near the middle of the line preceding or following it.

DACTYLIC

A combination of one stressed syllable followed by two unstressed syllables (DA da da DA da da DA da da). A pattern made up primarily of these dactyls is dactylic. Examples: loving it; puppy dog; tickle me.

DIMETER

A line consisting of two poetic feet (metric units), usually of a kind, as in two iambs or two anapests.

DRAMATIC

One of the three major genres of poetry. Dramatic poems place the action before the reader as does a play. See <u>Genre</u>.

END RHYME

Also terminal rhyme; what happens when rhymes occur at the ends of lines.

END-STOPPED

Lines that end on a pause are called end-stopped. Most poetic lines conclude with some sort of hesitation marked by punctuation, phrasing, or other natural pause.

FIXED FORM

Any poem that must fit a strictly defined set of rules. For examples see haiku, tanka, ballad, limerick, and Crapsey cinquain, listed alphabetically.

FOOT

A combination of syllables constituting a metrical unit in verse. The six most common poetic feet in the English language (iamb, anapest, trochee, dactyl, spondee, and pyrrhus) are listed alphabetically.

FREE VERSE

Poetry that is not "regular" enough to be called verse. Typically, free verse shows no formal devices of verse, such as meter or rhyme, yet it is free to do so at any point. But free verse has form enough to set it apart from mere prose. The poet must arrange the length of lines and select syllables and words that fit the desired mood and imagery.

FULL RHYME

Also called *true rhyme*, the relationship between words with identical vowel sounds, usually the last one accented, when the consonants immediately preceding are different and all vowels and consonants following sound the same. Examples: peach/preach; although/below; conserving/unnerving.

GENRE
Verse can be divided into three broad categories: <u>dramatic</u>, <u>narrative</u>, and <u>lyric</u>. Each is described in alphabetical order.

HAIKU
An unrhymed Japanese form that usually consists of 17 syllables, divided among three lines of 5, 7, and 5 syllables, respectively.

IAMBIC
A combination of one unstressed syllable followed by one stressed syllable (da DA da DA da DA). A pattern made up primarily of these iambs is iambic. Examples: delight; get up; enough; my friend.

INITIAL RHYME
Rhymes that occur at the beginnings of lines. Example:
> Nancy, in her party dress,
> Fancy as can be

INTERNAL RHYME
Rhymes that occur within the line. Most often the rhyming partner occurs at the end of the line, as in: A bear with no hair. Occasionally the rhyme occurs before the end of the line. Example: Let's go below before it storms.

LIMERICK
A five-line fixed form of light verse. Though often irregular, the goal is for the first, second, and fifth lines to be anapestic trimeter (three sets of da da DA); lines three and four to be anapestic dimeter (two sets of da da DA). The rhyme scheme is always *aabba*.

LINE
As prose moves in units of sentences and paragraphs, poetry moves in lines and groups of lines called stanzas. The line is a common feature of both verse and free verse and provides us a standard reference for study and measurement. In verse, the length of line is usually defined by the number of poetic feet (metrical units) it contains: one foot (monometer), two (dimeter), three (trimeter), four (tetrameter), etc.

LINK RHYME

Rhymes that occur when the last syllable of one line joins with the first sound or syllable of the next. Example (from *The Future Me* by David Harrison):

> Looking back, I see
> Me, unafraid,
> Eager, teasing,
> Pleasing, first grade.

LYRIC

One of three major categories of verse. (See *Genre*.) Lyric poetry was originally written to be sung (to the accompaniment of a lyre). The words of songs are still called lyrics. Now we call *lyric* anything that expresses personal feelings, real or imagined. Most poetry written today can be called lyric.

METAPHOR

"Saying one thing in terms of another" (Frost). Sometimes we distinguish between degrees of comparison, reserving metaphor for when we call one thing another, investing one thing or object with the usual characteristics of the other. "He's a rock."

METER

From the Greek word for measure. The pattern of a line, its specific and measurable characteristics, becomes its meter. Without words, there is still meter; we can peck it out on a tabletop with our fingertips.

NARRATIVE

One of three major categories of verse. (See *Genre*.) Narrative poems tell a story but not as directly "on stage" as dramatic poems do. They tend to summarize more and to describe action rather than participate in it.

NEAR RHYME

Also called slant rhyme, half rhyme, and off rhyme, these occur when part of one word echoes a sound in common with another. There are too many possibilities to categorize briefly. Alliteration, assonance, and consonance describe specific occurrences that are described in alphabetical order.

ONOMATOPOEIA

From the Greek word that means *name making:* Words that sound like what they represent, as in *pop, bang, whoosh.* Such descriptive sounds may have helped form early efforts to communicate.

PENTAMETER

A line consisting of five poetic feet or metrical units.

PICTURE POEM

Also concrete or spatial. Poems that use typography to construct a picture of their subject on the page.

POETRY

From the Greek word for *made up.* There are two major divisions of poetry: poems that are essentially metered (verse) and those that are primarily unmetered (free verse), both of which are described in alphabetical order. It's been said that poetry consists not so much in saying memorable things as in saying things memorably. More important than the subject is the way the poet uses language and form to express it.

PROSODY

The study of the physical aspects of poetry, including such details as meter, line, stanza, tempo, rhythm, sound, pause, rhyme, rhymelessness, color, pitch, and stress.

PYRRHIC

A combination of two syllables, both of which are unstressed (da da). The result is a pyrrhus, and it is sometimes used as a substitute for iambs (da DA) or trochees (DA da).

QUATRAIN

A stanza of four lines; the favorite English verse form. Of the eight most common types, three (regular, short, and long ballads) are included in this book and described in the glossary in alphabetical order.

RUN-ON LINE

Also called *runover* line or *enjambment*. This refers to a line that doesn't come to a natural pause at the end, which readers generally anticipate, but instead runs on into the next line. Such a line is intended to push us along more quickly into the following line.

RHYTHM

From the Greek word for *flow*. Rhythm is the total quality of a line's motion. Every line of poetry has its own rhythm, which we feel and interpret—as we do songs and dance—in personal ways.

SIMILE

From the Latin word for *like*. Comparing one thing to another to provide understanding or insight, as in, "Chocolate ice cream tastes like prunes/ ...Since Hanna moved away." (Judith Viorst)

SPONDAIC

A combination of two syllables, both of which are stressed (DA DA). The result is a spondee, and it is sometimes used as a substitute for iambs (da DA) or trochees (DA da). Examples: not fair; did not; did too.

STANZA

From the Italian word meaning *station* or *stopping place*. Refers to a group of lines that compose a pattern (such as number of feet per line or rhyme scheme) that is usually repeated.

STRESS

The English language is called a stress or *accentual* language because we place more emphasis on some syllables than on others. In any word of two syllables or more, at least one becomes dominant or stressed, as in domino, finger, special, women.

SYLLABLE

A unit of speech sound that consists of one or more distinctive sounds, called *phones*. A combination of letter(s) in a word set off from the rest of the word by the amount of stress it receives during pronunciation.

TANKA
An unrhymed Japanese form which has 31 syllables in five lines; essentially a haiku with a related couplet of 14 syllables following the first lines.

TERCET
Three lines rhyming consecutively are also called a *triplet*. If the rhyming forms an interlocking pattern, the stanza is also called a *Terza rima*.

TETRAMETER
A line consisting of four poetic feet or metrical units.

TRIMETER
A line consisting of three poetic feet or metrical units.

TROCHAIC
A combination of one stressed syllable followed by one unstressed syllable (DA da DA da DA da). A pattern made up primarily of these trochees is trochaic. Examples: dirty; water; kitten; mother; father.

VERSE
Structured or metered language. Free verse, by contrast, is unmetered language. What defines verse from free verse is its degree of regularity, its pattern of syllables and lines. Poetry that is too regular to be free verse is verse, whether it rhymes or not.

Acknowledgments

"When I Was Lost" by Dorothy Aldis. From *All Together* by Dorothy Aldis. Copyright 1925-1928, 1934, 1939, 1952 renewed 1953, © 1954-1956, 1962 by Dorothy Aldis. © 1967 by Roy Porter, renewed. Used by permission of G.P. Putnam's Sons, a division of Penguin Putnam, Inc.

"Wasps" by Dorothy Aldis. From *Is Anybody Hungry?* by Dorothy Aldis. Copyright © 1964 by Dorothy Aldis. Used by permission of G.P. Putnam's Sons, a division of Penguin Putnam Inc.

"First Snow" by Marie Louise Allen. Text copyright © 1957 by Marie Allen Howarth. Used by permission of HarperCollins Publishers.

"Beside the Line of Elephants" by Edna Becker. Reprinted by permission of The Caxton Printers, Ltd., Caldwell ID.

"The Music Master" by John Ciardi. Reprinted by permission of the estate of John Ciardi.

"Sea Gull" from *Summer Green* by Elizabeth Coatsworth. © 1947 by Macmillan Publishing Co., Inc., renewed 1975 by Elizabeth Coatsworth Beston.

"My Cat" by Barbara Juster Esbensen. Copyright © 1992 by Barbara Juster Esbensen. Used by permission of HarperCollins Publishers.

"Looking Down in the Rain" by Barbara Juster Esbensen. From *Cold Stars and Fireflies: Poems of the Four Seasons* by Barbara Juster Esbensen. Copyright © 1984 by Barbara Juster Esbensen. Used by permission of HarperCollins Publishers.

"Whee" written and designed by Robert Froman. Lettering by Ray Barber. From *Seeing Things: A Book of Poems*. Published by Thomas Y. Crowell Co., 1974.

"Some People" by Rachel Field. Reprinted by permission of Simon & Schuster Books for Young Readers, an imprint of Simon & Schuster Children's Publishing Division from *Poems* by Rachel Field (Macmillan, NY 1957).

"The Lizard" by John Gardner. From *A Child's Beastiary* by John Gardner. Copyright © 1977 by Boskydell Artists Ltd. Reprinted by permission of Georges Borchardt, Inc.

"Polliwogs" by Kristine O'Connell George. From *The Great Frog Race and Other Poems* by Kristine O'Connell George. Copyright © 1997. Published by Houghton Mifflin, 1997. Used by permission of the publisher.

"Walking to Church" by Monica Gunning. From *Not A Copper Penny In Me House* by Monica Gunning. © 1993 by Monica Gunning. Published by Wordsong/Boyds Mills Press, Inc.

"Fishes" by Georgia Heard from *Creatures of the Earth, Sea, and Sky* by Georgia Heard. Published by Wordsong/Boyds Mills Press, Inc. Reprinted by permission.